The Art of
Preserved Flower
Arrangement

Maureen Foster

The Art of
Preserved Flower
Arrangement

Collins

I would like to dedicate this book to my husband,
whose beautifully clear and concise illustrations con-
tributed so much, not only to the practical appeal of
this book but to all my previous books as well, and
whose encouragement has helped me to survive the
sometimes depressing aspects of producing a book.

First published in 1984
by William Collins Sons & Co Ltd
8 Grafton Street, London W1X 3LA
Glasgow, Sydney, Auckland, Johannesburg

All arrangements illustrated are the author's original
work.
All photographs and line drawings by Bryan Foster.

ISBN 0 00 411625 9

Text set in Century Schoolbook
by Advanced Filmsetters (Glasgow) Ltd
Printed and bound in Spain
by Graficromo SA Cordoba

Contents

Introduction

In writing this, my sixth book dealing with preservation and the use of preserved plant materials, I have once again felt the privilege of sharing with others, through words and photographs, my love of working with the colours, textures and shapes from nature's vast treasure trove. I hope my ideas will continue to inspire my readers and also encourage new readers to experiment with this fascinating art form, and to discover the joy and pleasure of working with preserved plant materials.

It is now eleven years since the publication of my first book, **Preserved Flowers— Practical Methods and Creative Uses**. In most of my published work since that time I have concentrated on specialized aspects of preserving, such as **Creating Pictures with Preserved Flowers** and **Making Animal and Bird Collages with Grasses, Leaves and Cones**. However, I feel from the many letters and inquiries I receive that many readers find that although they have large and varied collections of preserved flowers and foliage and a longing to make preserved flower arrangements to enhance their own homes, they do not quite know what to put with what. Preserved arrangements can today be far more versatile than the traditional neatly filled pots of everlasting flowers—pretty though these often are. Today it is possible to create a preserved arrangement in the style of a fresh arrangement, and by using a wide range of preserved plant materials we can defy that label 'typically dried'. For me the ultimate joy of flower preserving is to be able to produce an arrangement in a particular colour scheme, at a particular time, for a particular occasion or purpose. I am delighted that Collins have given me this opportunity to illustrate in colour a book of ideas for preserving and arranging preserved flowers in the home, with emphasis on the harmonious colour effects that it is possible to create, particularly when blending preserved plant materials with furnishings.

For arrangers who wish to experiment with colour effects, preserved flowers are a great asset. We can choose from all the seasons of the year. And once a selection of colours has been preserved, time can be spent arranging and rearranging and learning the effects that can be created—often with colours we may not previously have considered using together. I hope that both amateur and experienced flower arrangers will find in this book ideas which can be adapted to their individual needs. For even the most experienced flower arrangers, while happy to spend a considerable amount of time and effort arranging flowers for a flower festival or some other charitable event, may feel that they cannot afford to spend so much time creating for the home arrangements which will only last for a brief period. However, if the time is invested in creating a preserved arrangement it will pay dividends, as instead of lasting a few days or even a week the arrangement will remain in good condition for at the very least a few months.

I am often asked questions such as 'Do you grow all the flowers?' and 'Do you have a large garden to grow all these flowers?' and 'Do you grow special flowers for preserving?' The answer to all these questions is 'No!' We have a garden of average size, planted to give visual interest all the year round. If you analyze the colour plates you will find that most of my arrangements are composed of ordinary garden flowers, foliage and seedheads that are common in most gardens. However, there is always something that I am needing which I don't happen to grow, but a kind friend does, and of course in season many flowers are inexpensive at the florist's or in the local market. The reader who has only a town flat and no garden need not feel that flower preserving is out of reach; a day out to a friend's garden, or to collect common wild plant materials from the hedgerows, or even just a visit to purchase a few blooms from a florist's or a street barrow can provide many months of lasting enjoyment.

For readers who feel that you cannot be a flower arranger without a large cupboard crammed with elegant vases, I have illustrated how to adapt inexpensive items for use as containers. I have also shown how to apply paint to plastic containers to create an antique effect and enable a more pleasing harmony to be created between plant materials and container.

It has always been a great joy to me to work in miniature and I know many readers will feel the same way, so I have devoted a chapter of my book to a small selection of ideas for petite and miniature arrangements. It is easier and I feel more rewarding to create a tiny arrangement with preserved plant materials, since no water is needed.

Imported, made-up or contrived 'flowers' are very costly, and after all they are only the work of observant people who are able to see the beauty of shape and form in their native plant materials, and who simply and effectively assemble plant parts to form attractive flower-like shapes. For the price of a tube of glue you can become a plant hybridizer and dream up your own unique flowers. In Chapter 5 I have shared with you my secrets for making some of my own simple 'fun flowers', as I like to call them.

Flowers traditionally play an important part in celebrations: in Chapter 6 I describe how preserved flowers can be used to enhance a variety of special occasions.

Because flowers and other plant materials differ so in structure, substance, colour and texture, it is not possible to preserve them all in the same way, but is necessary to use different methods of preserving. These methods are described and illustrated in the reference section at the end of the book. The plant materials I have used in each arrangement are identified in the diagrams accompanying the photographs. On page 138 all the plants are listed in alphabetical order, and reference is made to the most effective method of preservation.

Maureen Foster, Wilton, 1984

1 The beauty of preserved foliage

Foliage, more than any other plant material, lifts a preserved arrangement out of the class of arrangements dismissed as 'typically Victorian'. An arrangement with foliage has much more appeal for most modern flower arrangers. I have often heard arrangers of fresh flowers say that if they had to choose between flowers and foliage they would always choose foliage. Carefully selected foliage plays an even more important part in preserved arrangements. While many fresh flowers have a few leaves on their stems, with preserved flowers the stems are usually completely bare; more often than not, indeed, the stems have to be discarded and replaced by covered wires. Even the most experienced flower arranger will have difficulty in creating effective preserved arrangements—other than modern line arrangements—without so much as a single leaf. But as you will see in plate 2, quite an effective arrangement can be created from foliage without a single flower. This arrangement relies on carefully chosen leaf forms and contrasting leaf colourings.

Plate 1 This arrangement shows how preserved plant materials can be used to complement and harmonize with an ornament. Preserved water lilies are arranged with their own leaves and graceful tiny-leaved sprays of silver birch. Some of the water lily leaves have their undersides uppermost, so that the subtle pink colour on the edges of the undersides is visible. The eye is drawn to the water lilies by the figurine. Restraint is the keynote of this arrangement, as the delicate colourings of the beautiful figures would be completely overpowered if they were positioned within a mass of plant material.

Foliage colour

Preserved foliage in fact carries a bonus for the flower arranger. By exploiting the different methods of preservation, the range of foliage colourings available to the arranger can be greatly extended. For example, many shades of brown and yellow are a direct result of preserving mature green leaves by the glycerine method (plates 3 and 4). In contrast, the beautiful lime-green colourings of many young, immature leaves of spring and early summer can be successfully preserved by desiccants (see plate 21). The gorgeous rich reds of autumn leaves can also be captured by the desiccant method—a particular delight, as when fresh these are so beautiful, but, alas, for such a short time, only to be swept away by the autumn gales and forgotten until autumn comes again (plate 5).

Foliage should be carefully chosen to accentuate the colour scheme of an arrangement. In the arrangement illustrated in plate 15, for example, the olive green of Solomon's Seal leaves highlights the colour of the centres of the delphiniums. In plate 75 a few dark brown glycerined forsythia leaves not only provide a link with the dark brown velvet of the shell base but also help to intensify the gold colouring of the preserved flowers, as green foliage would not have done.

Leaf shape

Anyone who has made an attempt to preserve plant materials will almost certainly at some time or other have preserved beech leaves. I find it difficult to understand why

Plate 2 An empty wine bottle holds a colourful arrangement of contrasting leaf forms: mahonia (1), escallonia (2), mountain ash (3), choisya (4), *Cineraria maritima* (5) and ivy (6). The desiccant method was used to capture and preserve the colourings of the mountain ash, *Cineraria maritima* and ivy leaves, the glycerine method for the mahonia, escallonia and choisya leaves.

10

beech foliage should be so popular, as the leaves are rather an uninteresting shape. There is such a range of trees and shrubs which produce more distinctively shaped leaves. It is possible for the observant arranger to preserve a wide variety of leaves, which can provide a contrast to flowers in shape as well as colour. A selection of differently shaped leaves is illustrated in plates 3 and 4.

Plates 3 and 4 A selection of foliage preserved by the glycerine method, showing the two distinct groups of foliage colourings produced. Except for the *Eleagnus pungens*, all the foliage was green when fresh.

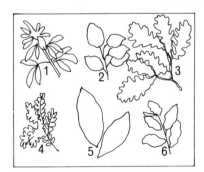

Plate 3 Choisya (1), *Eleagnus x ebbingei* (2), oak (3), box (4), Solomon's Seal (5), *Eleagnus pungens* (6).

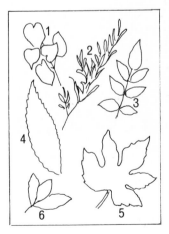

Plate 4 Epimedium (1), *Danae racemosa* (2), mahonia (3), sweet chestnut (4), fatsia (5), *Helleborus orientalis* (6).

11

Plate 5 Red autumn leaves, showing the varying shades from red to deep burgundy. These leaves were all preserved by the desiccant method. The collection also illustrates some of the many interesting leaf formations.

Plate 6 These leaves were all picked in late October and early November and arranged in January. I captured the sycamore leaf colourings while some leaves were still green and others had changed to yellow. The beautiful dark red mountain ash leaves I gathered from under the tree immediately they had fallen, while those that had only just changed from green to red I picked from the tree. These were a much lighter red and made into fun flowers—with doronicum seedhead centres—they provided contrast in both colour and form. A few poppy seedheads provide additional interest in this flowerless but colourful arrangement.

Leaves with interesting markings

The possibilities of leaves with distinctive markings are often overlooked by the arranger of preserved flowers. The hosta leaves in plate 7 make a simple but effective arrangement with a restful effect. If stored immediately after preserving, rich multi-green herbaceous leaves such as these can be arranged out of season, to give several months of pleasure during the winter. I regret to say that as with most green foliage the colouring will in time slowly fade, but the leaves will still be very useful in arrangements which require more subdued colourings.

All the leaves in this group should be preserved by the desiccant method.

Silver foliage

Silver foliage is very precious to the flower arranger who enjoys delicate and pretty colour schemes. An arrangement of blue flowers is enhanced by silver foliage, and for pink arrangements silver foliage is almost a must. Plate 8 illustrates a concentrated blending of mauve and cerise flowers. A little silver added in the form of foliage prevents the arrangement from becoming too solid-looking, and also provides a link with the silver candlestick. In fact silver foliage is an obvious choice when any form of silver container is used for preserved flowers. In an all-foliage arrangement a few carefully selected silver leaves will prove a contrast to darker-coloured foliage. I always feel the range of useful silver leaves suitable for preserving is more limited than that of any other colour, although I never really experience any difficulty in finding just the right size and type of silver foliage for an arrangement. *Cineraria maritima* is my favourite silver plant, as it produces quite large, mature leaves which have a wonderful sculptured quality, and even the tiny immature leaves that form in the centre of the plant remain firm and rigid after preserving and are ideal for miniature arrangements.

Plate 7 The elegant shape of the carved horn heron was the inspiration for the form of this simple arrangement using two different leaf forms. The colours harmonize with those of the curtain fabric. I picked *Hosta fortunei* early in the season to capture the extraordinary marbled effect of the leaves, which later change to plain green. Strap-like leaves of montbretia contrast with the hosta leaves. The floral clay pressed into a black plastic dish to hold the flowers also serves as an anchorage for the heron.

15

Plate 9 A selection of silver foliage. Artemisia (1), *Chrysanthemum haradjanii* (2), *Cineraria maritima* (3), *Stachys lanata* (4), *Senecio greyi* (5), common white-beam (6), echinops (7), *Stachys lanata* calyces with small leaves attached (8), *Eleagnus x ebbingei*, with the undersides of the leaves showing (9).

Plate 8 This colour scheme of cerise and mauve was planned in early summer and the flowers were collected, preserved and stored during the summer months and arranged in the autumn. A silver container is a perfect accompaniment for cerise. Silver foliage, uniting flowers and candlestick, was an obvious choice, but to retain the impact of the colour the foliage was used with restraint. The flowers used were roses (1), rambler roses 'Dorothy Perkins' (2), fuchsias (3), statice (4), astilbe (5), hydrangeas (6) and spray chrysanthemums (7), with *Cineraria maritima* (8), eucalyptus (9) and *Chrysanthemum haradjanii* foliage (10), and silver buds of *Senecio greyi* (11).

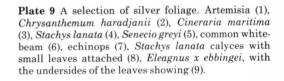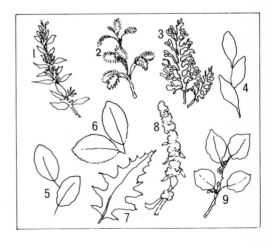

Wiring leaves

It is often useful to wire leaves to provide them with longer stems. 20-gauge florists' wires are the best to use, if you can get them, but it is frequently only possible to buy small standard packs of florists' wires. You will need to check that the wires are rigid and sturdy enough to support the leaves. Secure the wire to the stem with florists' fine silver wire or reel wire, as shown in fig. 1a. Wiring can also be a good way of making one branch of leaves sufficient for a complete arrangement. Just cut all the leaves from the main stem, complete with their leaf stalks, and wire them individually as shown in fig. 1b. Plate 60 illustrates how interesting effects can be achieved by making individual leaves into sprays to suit a particular style of arrangement. The great advantage of this is that each spray can be bent to whatever angle the arranger desires (fig. 1c).

If the wires are likely to show in the finished arrangement they should be bound with florists' tape, in the same way as flowers (see page 23).

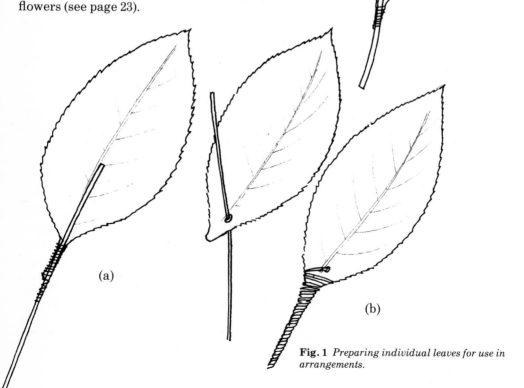

(a)

(b)

(c)

Fig. 1 *Preparing individual leaves for use in arrangements.*

18

2 Creating harmonious effects with preserved flowers

Chapter 1 illustrates that attractive preserved arrangements can be created using foliage alone, and in fact plant materials of all kinds have their part to play. But in creating colour effects, particularly effects that harmonize with furnishings, it is, in the majority of preserved arrangements, flowers that play the most important role, with foliage being used to intensify or complement their colouring.

Throughout the year, fresh flowers are gathered and enjoyed in their season: snowdrops in February, daffodils in March, roses in June. The keen gardener may ask why he should be interested in preserved flower arrangements when he can produce flowers for a fresh arrangement at any time of the year. However, this is to miss the point. Preserved flowers are not a substitute for fresh flowers. A preserved flower arrangement is perhaps best regarded as a detail of the interior decoration. It can be used to create or reinforce a particular effect, whether of elegance or casual charm.

Most preserved arrangements are created for the home. And we can all find a position in a room which would be enhanced by the introduction of a preserved arrangement with a carefully chosen blending of colour. The collecting and preserving of plant materials can be done at leisure over a period of weeks or even months, when weather conditions permit. In this way plant materials not only in different shapes and forms but also from different seasons can be preserved and used in harmony with each other—provided that a degree of restraint is exercised. For example, daffodils somehow could not be considered as ideal partners for roses; but early summer flowering peonies and hydrangeas preserved in autumn complement each other perfectly. With preserved flowers all the seasons of the year are at once available. If we also accept the changes of tone that take place in some flowers during the preserving process, still more possibilities are opened up. So whatever the style and colour scheme of a room it is possible at any time of the year to create an arrangement that is in harmony.

New students are often inclined to preserve a large number of flowers with little thought as to their ultimate use. This is not a bad approach for the beginner, because there is nothing like practice to perfect the art of preserving flowers, and there is no better way of learning to understand the types of flowers that may or may not be suitable for preserving. But as progress is made more thought should be given to the end product. If you intend using flowers for an arrangement in your own home you must take into consideration the room in which you plan to arrange the flowers. At this stage I would recommend making your choice of flowers for preserving with a particular arrangement in mind. You will be surprised to discover how few desiccant-preserved flowers are necessary to create an impact of colour within an arrangement. It is often necessary to use only three, five or seven flowers as centres of interest. Ideal for this purpose are roses, lilies, carnations, peonies, dahlias or rudbeckias, depending of course on the size of the arrangement.

Preserving flowers

The question often arises of how best to preserve the different types of flowers. This is a relatively easy decision to make once what happens when a flower is preserved is clearly understood. When plant material is preserved in a glycerine mixture the glycerine keeps the structure soft and pliable, but a marked colour change is apparent. If flowers are preserved by this method, their colour, the quality of which is so important to us, will be lost. The only way of keeping the colour is to remove the moisture from the flowers. Obviously, preserved in this way a flower will not have the same resilience as glycerine-preserved material, and with its somewhat fragile structure it will need careful handling, but I consider this a small price to pay for such rewarding results. Now let us consider what happens when we remove the moisture from a flower, which is really exactly what nature does as the flower in the garden dies. To observe exactly how a flower dies will serve as a useful guide to the best method by which to extract the moisture from that flower. For example, flowers, such as roses, with distinct petal shapes will wither and the petals will curl up or fall as they die. Flowers which have this type of structure need to be preserved in a desiccant which will hold the actual shape and form of each petal while it extracts the moisture (see page 143). On the other hand, a flowering head of achillea consists of many tiny, closely packed florets without distinct petal shapes; as it dies, the colour fades with the constant light, but the structure remains the same. Flowers which have a structure similar to that of the achillea can be preserved by the natural or air method (see page 157). Again, most flowers with petaloid sepals can, when they are mature, be preserved naturally. These plants have tiny, insignificant flowers surrounded by large, often colourful petaloid sepals (petaloid means resembling a petal), which form the calyces of the flowers and persist long after the real flowers have withered. If you inspect a hydrangea flower during the summer you will see what I mean. Towards autumn these petaloid sepals mature and become firm, and their colours change. Pale pinks turn a lovely green, while darker pinks turn a beautiful, rich, almost mahogany red, and bright blues become a more subdued shade of steel blue. At this stage they are almost papery to the touch and can be preserved naturally. There are other flowers where instead of being petal-like the sepals are joined and envelop each individual floret in the form of a bell or a trumpet shape. Good examples of such plants are the moluccella (Bells of Ireland) and the balotta. Here again, it is the mature calyces which can be preserved by the air method. It is important to remember that immature calyces can only be successfully preserved by desiccants.

Flowers of the group known as everlasting flowers or straw flowers are easily preserved by the air method. These flowers with characteristically papery petals or bracts grow wild in warmer climates but in Britain must be cultivated as half-hardy annuals. Perhaps the best known of the everlastings are the helichrysum and the statice. Although when they are gathered together in a mixed bunch the colours of these flowers are rather harsh, individually selected colours are ideal to combine with other flowers of the same shade, often helping to accentuate a particular colour in an arrangement (see plate 13).

While it is fun to preserve rare, unusual or exotic flowers, to learn to look and to observe the infinite beauty of many of the more common flowers can be so rewarding. Preserving flowers can actually help arrangers to do just this. I can recall many students who after attending my flower-preserving sessions have remarked on the fact that they have learnt more than just how to preserve flowers. Until that time they had not appreciated the beauty of many of the quite common flowers that grew in their gardens or in the countryside round them, flowers often dismissed as weeds.

In plate 17 on page 32 you will see an arrangement made from ground elder. This is a despised weed but its flowers resemble an exquisite tracery of lace.

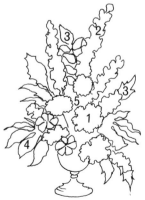

Plate 10 Yellow achillea (1) and Bells of Ireland (2) arranged against a background of the beautiful leaf formations of mahonia (3) and fatsia (4), with a few almost black leaves of aucuba (5) recessed between the achillea heads. I feel the bronze urn is very much in harmony with these plant materials.

Plate 11 A preserved wedding buttonhole. Because its fleshy texture made the preserving process so long-winded, it was not possible to preserve the true pale pink colour of this Cymbidium orchid; however, its shape and form and even the beautiful markings have been retained. Arranged in a recessed frame lined with cream silk, it makes a keepsake to be treasured. The tiny variegated ivy leaves which were part of the buttonhole have preserved particularly successfully.

Preserving the exotics

Tropical plants can present a particular problem from the point of view of preservation. These plants often have thick, fleshy petals which enable them to conserve moisture and withstand the long periods of drought to which their natural habitat subjects them. Of course, the thicker the petals of a flower, the longer the flower takes to preserve. Orchids of the larger-flowered varieties, for example, can take three weeks or more. This usually results in the loss of much of the flower's colour. So these are certainly not the flowers to choose if you want to create a colourful arrangement. However, if an orchid is preserved for sentimental reasons, as they so often are, it can

Plate 12 While many artificial flowers at first sight give the impression that they are fresh flowers, to me the strange waxy forms of anthurium flowers actually look artificial. But somehow they are always so appealing to the arranger who is in search of something different. I think I actually prefer the preserved chocolate brown colouring of these once red anthuriums, the gift of a florist friend in Madeira. Here they are arranged on a cardboard base with a few beautifully marked pieces of rock and an interesting piece of driftwood, all of which found their way into my suitcase when we returned from holiday. I soaked the driftwood for about an hour in neat domestic bleach.

serve as a happy reminder of a memorable occasion. And because of the firm structure of the petals, the orchid's interesting shape and form are maintained after it is preserved (plate 11).

The anthurium's thick, waxy spathes present the same difficulty as the petals of the orchid; in fact the anthuriums in plate 12, which were originally dark red, took a whole month to preserve, but their architectural qualities made them well worth preserving. Actually, I find their chocolate brown colour quite pleasing.

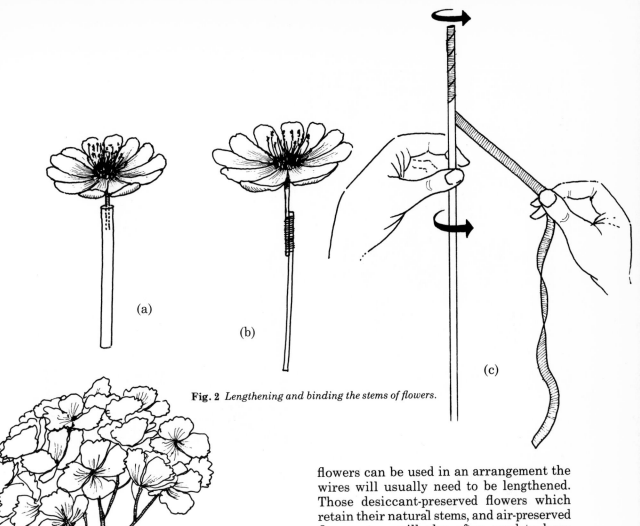

(a)

(b)

(c)

Fig. 2 *Lengthening and binding the stems of flowers.*

(d)

Lengthening flower stems

Many flowers that are preserved in a desiccant need to be wired before preservation. Instructions for this preliminary wiring are given in the reference section (page 144). For practical reasons only short wires are used at this initial stage, but before the flowers can be used in an arrangement the wires will usually need to be lengthened. Those desiccant-preserved flowers which retain their natural stems, and air-preserved flowers too, will also often need to have their stems lengthened before they can be arranged effectively.

Hollow plant stalks from grasses or other wild herbaceous plants can sometimes be used as extension stems. Dab a little glue on the end of the flower stem and carefully insert it in the hollow stalk (fig. 2a).

Usually, however, you will need to use wires to lengthen the stems. Secure the wire to the stem with florists' fine silver wire or reel wire (fig. 2b). Extending a stem with wire has the great advantage that it is possible to bend each stem to suit the angle at which you wish to use it in an arrangement. It is advisable to bind the wired stem, to hide the join and to provide the smooth wire with a firmer means of anchorage in an arrangement. For competitive work, of course, this is essential. Narrow plastic tape made especially for the purpose can be bought from florists. Several different brands of tape are available, and though they vary slightly, they all work in basically the same way. Figure 2c shows how to hold the stem and twist the tape round it. Provided that the tape is kept taut it will adhere to itself and to the wire or plant stem. Press with your fingertips, especially at the start and finish of binding, to make sure it sticks firmly.

Many large flower heads, such as those of the hydrangea, consist of not one but many branched stems, each bearing numerous small florets (fig. 2d). If you lengthen each little stem, either with a hollow stalk or a wire, you will be able to use the sections separately.

valuable for their impressive architectural quality and interesting texture.

Seedcases that are to be used purely for their interesting forms and architectural quality can be harvested after they have released their seeds, when nature has already dried many of them to an almost wood-like texture. In fact, many seedcases are more attractive shapes after they have opened to release their seeds. On the other hand, the same seedheads at an earlier stage, just as they approach maturity but before the seeds ripen, will often reveal interesting textures and subtle colourings, and many have particularly beautiful markings too. If they are harvested at this stage, their colour value can be as great an asset in an arrangement as their shape.

The remarkable structure of seedheads

As a general rule, most of the colour in a preserved flower arrangement is of course provided by flowers and foliage. And the successful preservation of most flowers and leaves entails the use of glycerine or desiccants. Fortunately, although these plant materials are valuable for their colour, it is often only necessary to use them in small quantities. Seedheads, which are easily dried by the air method (see page 157), can provide contrast of shape and form for use in both outlining an arrangement and filling in—supplying transitional material. Spiky seedheads on long stems are ideal to give height to an arrangement; and pendulous seedheads will provide graceful, arching sprays to trail over the edge of a pedestal-type container, giving a downward flow. The formation of many seedheads, such as the artichoke seedhead illustrated in fig. 27, is really quite remarkable. I have chosen to dissect artichoke seedheads and use the parts to make interesting and unusual contrived flowers—fun flowers, as I call them (see plates 57, 58 and 59). Arrangers who enjoy creating line arrangements will find the complete seedheads in-

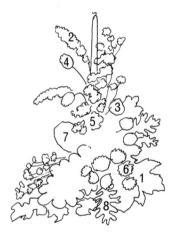

Plate 13 The unusual colour effect of this arrangement was woven round the candle and the bunch of artificial grapes. The only desiccant-preserved materials here are the copper-coloured leaves. It is difficult to believe that this is the true colour of very young sycamore leaves (1), gathered in the spring. The calyces of *Stachys lanata* (2) and the seedheads of love-in-a-mist (3) and poppy (4) were chosen for their colouring. I used purple marjoram (5) and helichrysum (6), together with smoke tree leaves (7), to introduce the necessary depth of purple. The serrated silver leaves are *Cineraria maritima* (8).

24

Holiday treasures

To all but the dedicated flower arranger, this heading may at first appear strangely out of place in a book on flower preserving and arranging. I will explain. For many arrangers, like myself, holidays are the one time of year when we can walk freely and at leisure, with the time and opportunity to explore new areas of countryside and seashore. The traveller abroad has the additional interest of observing and studying plants and trees with which he may not be familiar. It is equally exciting when you discover that species of plants which may be cultivated in your own garden are in fact natives of the country you are visiting. I hesitate to suggest picking any wild plant materials wherever we live or travel, and I do so with certain reservations. I must emphasize that many countries have protected species of plants; these, of course, should not be picked. It is worth inquiring whether any such laws exist before you gather any plant materials. It is, however, encouraging to know that it is usually the more common flowers and seedheads that are the most successfully preserved and these are unlikely to be among the protected species. There are also in many countries regulations about importing plants. If you wish to bring entire plants (including the roots) into Britain, before you go abroad you must apply to the Ministry of Agriculture for information about any restrictions on imports from the countries you plan to visit. There should be no problem, however, with cut plant materials which I have brought into the country many times.

The acanthus in plate 14 was found growing wild in Greece. The driftwood here has a special meaning too and will always be treasured, as it will be with me long after the preserved flowers have been consigned to the dustbin. In the future whenever I use this piece of gnarled olive wood it will bring back memories of my holiday and especially the leisurely hours spent in the dappled sunlight among the olive groves.

Inevitably, the limited space available for transporting foreign materials will restrict such a collection, but for arrangements such as the one illustrated it is only necessary to gather a small quantity of material.

Plate 14 Four small spikes of *Acanthus spinosus* (1), the mauve of their bracts emphasized by the small mauve allium heads (2), are arranged with *Helichrysum siculum* (3) and the spiky heads of *Phlomis fruticosa* (4) round a piece of old gnarled olive wood. *Acanthus spinosus* is a plant known in Greece since ancient times—its leaves are to be found in Greek designs dating from the third century BC. I chose a greeny-grey slate base, to give an impression of my holiday island's natural landscape. I did not bring the naturally dried moss back from my holiday, but I think it represents well the lush green of the island's vegetation.

Plate 16 Flowers which have become faded after several years of use take on a new role. The faded colourings of dahlias (1), zinnias (2) and rambler roses 'Dorothy Perkins' (3), used here with quaking grasses (4) and montbretia seedheads (5), tone beautifully with the shell container. *Viburnum tinus* foliage (6) makes an ideal foil for the flowers.

Plate 15 The impact of colour in this arrangement of delphiniums (1) in their varying shades of blue is reinforced by the restricted use of foliage. The olive green of the individually wired leaves of Solomon's Seal (2) highlights the centres of the delphiniums. *Cineraria maritima* (3) and montbretia leaves (4) add contrast of form. The colouring of the bunch of artificial grapes seemed a perfect accompaniment to the leaves and also to the mottled grey of the plastic dish.

Containers for preserved arrangements

Almost anything may be used as a container for preserved flowers: a rare and exquisite piece of porcelain, an earthenware mug or a modern plastic dish. As there is no water, chipped or cracked containers or even containers with holes (provided the holes do not show) can be used. And attractively shaped cardboard boxes can be covered or painted to harmonize with a particular colour scheme.

There are three points to note when choosing a container that will be visible when the arrangement has been completed. First, the container should be appropriate to the furnishings of the room in which the

29

finished arrangement is to be displayed. Secondly, it should be of the right proportions for the position it is intended to occupy. And, thirdly, the most important point of all—if a pleasing arrangement is to be achieved, the container must harmonize with the plant materials. All this means careful consideration of the container's colour, shape, texture and size.

Many arrangements are designed in such a way that the container is not visible when the arrangement has been completed. You could consider using an empty tin as a container for such an arrangement. Small tins are particularly useful when more than one placement is necessary—for example, when flowers are arranged round a figurine. A block of flower foam can be fixed in the tin to hold the flowers. Naturally, it is more professional to paint the tin, especially if the arrangement is intended as a present. If it is for your own use, then I say, why bother! After all, it is not going to show, and as no water is used it is certainly not going to rust.

Inexpensive plastic dishes which are designed to take individual blocks of flower foam (fig. 3a) are readily available from florists. As the foam fits firmly and securely, there is no need for any additional anchorage. If necessary the dish can be painted a more desirable colour—the matt surface of the plastic takes paint well.

Empty wine bottles of all shapes and sizes can be adapted to take preserved arrangements. Plate 2 shows preserved foliage arranged in a wine bottle. Metal cup-shaped holders fitted with a spike designed to push into the cork of a bottle or the top of a candlestick can be bought (fig. 3b), but an alternative holder can easily be made at home—just stick the cork of the bottle to a tin lid of a suitable size (fig. 3c).

Holding plant materials in the container

Readers who are familiar with fresh flower arranging will no doubt have used the green plastic flower foam sold by florists under

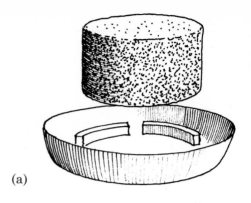

(a)

Fig. 3 *Preparing various types of containers with flower foam.*

(b)

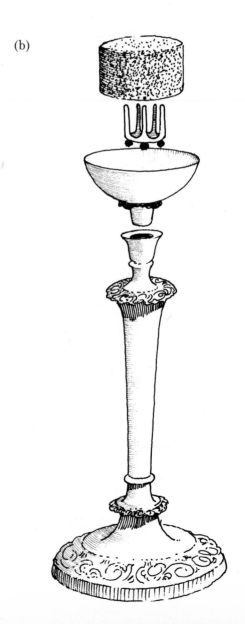

(c)

(d)

(e)

(f)

various trade names, such as Oasis. Used dry, this foam is also perfectly suitable for arrangements of preserved flowers, and in the past I used it in preference to the special foam that was then sold for preserved work. However, the new foam for preserved flowers which has come on the market in recent years is ideal, and I would advise using this if at all possible. It looks similar in texture to the fresh flower foam but is usually grey in colour, and it is much stronger. Both types of foam are available in small individual round or square blocks and large oblong blocks. The large blocks are usually more economical, as pieces can be cut to the exact size of containers (fig. 3d). A piece of flower foam cut to size can often be wedged into a container quite securely, without any danger of its becoming dislodged after the arrangement has been completed (fig. 3e). But if an arrangement is to be made directly on a base or in a shallow dish, some additional form of anchorage will be necessary. There are heavy metal holders with widely spaced prongs specially made to take blocks of flower foam, but although these are ideal they can be rather expensive. Small, inexpensive, reusable plastic four-pin prongs, which are readily available, provide a perfectly adequate substitute (fig. 3f). Either type of holder can be anchored firmly to a dry container by tiny pellet-shaped pieces of a sticky, putty-like substance which is sold by florists for this purpose. This florists' fixative can usually be purchased in lengths from 150 mm (6 in) upwards. Oasisfix is a well known brand. Alternatively, Plasticine can be used, but I would not rely on its holding power with a large arrangement, or heavy plant materials. If you are arranging heavy plant materials in a large, deep container, it is advisable to use crumpled 50 mm (2 in) wire netting, or chicken wire as it is often called, in the container, to hold the stems. A small grouping of plant materials arranged with driftwood can be held in place in a lump of Plasticine or floral clay, which should be moulded and anchored firmly in position before the plant materials are arranged.

Plate 17 It is easy to see how the umbelliferous wild plants that bloom throughout the summer acquired their shared common name of Queen Anne's Lace. For preserving, the plant I like best among this group is ground elder, as it has firm stems which support the flower when it has been preserved.

Plate 18 An empty brown plastic container with its top cut off holds a simple arrangement of white daisies and green ferns. I used a small chunk of flower foam pushed into the hole to hold my arrangement. There are many similar plastic containers to be found on the shelves of your local supermarket. I must confess, we occasionally find ourselves using a product simply because I am attracted to the container for preserved flowers!

Plate 19 Chippings of broken windscreen glass hold these three preserved water lilies in place in their glass dish. Easy to arrange with their own foliage, water lilies make an effective and striking display in winter. Broken windscreen glass is extremely useful for holding and concealing stems in glass containers. If you are not unlucky enough to be able to collect any from a broken windscreen of your own, a lay-by is a good place to look for it.

Plate 20 A carefully preserved specimen bloom can be stored and brought out on special occasions. This peony, with its wonderful colour and its sculptured quality, is particularly beautiful. The preserved foliage of the peony is arranged round the flower.

33

Painting containers for antique effect

I really enjoy painting containers to achieve an antique appearance. I find the finished effect so rewarding. Inexpensive plastic containers are readily available from florists, stores and garden centres. They are usually well made and attractive in shape, but they so often have that typically plastic look. Also, most of these mass-produced containers are rather drab and uninteresting in colour. But a quite ordinary modern container can be transformed by a little paint into an object which fits happily into a setting with antique furniture, and also looks an integral part of an arrangement, not just a container with flowers in it. I always use paints which will not wash off, so that the containers can be used for fresh flowers as well as preserved ones.

The basic idea is something for which I owe thanks to my friend Mr Fred Burdock. It is now many years since Mr Burdock showed me how he painted a figurine to give an antique appearance and I must say that I found my first efforts far from satisfactory. However, through experimenting and practising I soon found I could produce effects which were pleasing to me and then I began using the technique on containers. I now realize that although my tutor had been very patient in showing me how he applied paint to figurines, I needed to find my own technique that worked for me; I hope that in turn my readers, after being guided initially by my instructions, will go on to develop their own techniques and achieve their own individual effects.

Overleaf are directions for applying paint to a container such as the one shown in plate 22, with an embossed or raised surface pattern. One word of warning: this is definitely a job which should be reserved for a quiet evening when you are unlikely to be disturbed.

Plate 21 Here the plant materials and the container were carefully chosen to create an arrangement of elegance and charm. The white container is an old candlestick which has been repaired and adapted to take the arrangement. To relieve the flat white colouring a little raw umber oil paint was rubbed into the crevices. Green and white is one of my favourite colour schemes, though it is one which is rarely associated with preserved plant materials. Ballota (1) and alchemilla (2) are used to outline the shape of the arrangement and form a background for sprays of feverfew (3), dahlias (4), helichrysums (5) and individually wired hollyhock flowers (6). Desiccant-preserved green sycamore leaves (7) are recessed between the flowers.

You will need the following materials (fig. 4a):

A small, stiff brush, for example an artist's oil painting brush;
Oil paints—I used raw umber, Naples yellow and sap green. There are two grades of oil paints available, Artists' and Students'. Either grade is quite suitable for this type of work, but it is worth remembering that Students' colours are considerably cheaper;
White spirit for cleaning your brush.

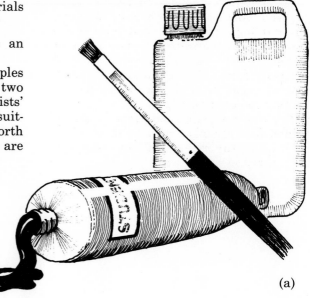

(a)

Brush raw umber straight from the tube roughly into the crevices (fig. 4b). Mix together Naples yellow and sap green and brush this colour over the raised parts. Some of this colour will merge into the raw umber, but the raw umber will still show in the deeper parts of the crevices. At this stage the container will probably look very messy, and you may feel like giving up, but don't worry, the next stage puts it all right.

Fig. 4 *Painting a container to create an antique effect.*

(b)

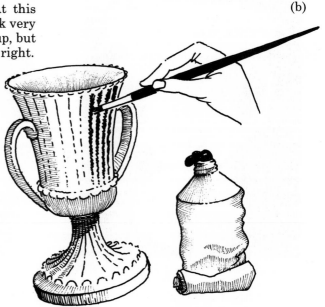

Cover your forefinger with a soft piece of rag and, holding the cloth taut, rub your covered finger over the raised parts of the container, concentrating on one section at a time (fig. 4c). This will remove much of the paint from these raised areas, leaving just a smear to give the container its creamy-coloured highlighting.

To cover the smooth, flat parts of the container, first roughly brush on raw umber, then brush the mixture of sap green and Naples yellow over the top.

(c)

Plate 22 A white plastic urn.

Plate 23 The same urn, after it has been painted.

Fig. 5 *The figurine here is not integrated into the arrangement.*

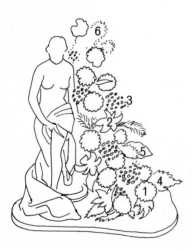

Plate 24 The inspiration for this arrangement came from the figurine and the fabric. I chose the rich shades of Pompon dahlias (1) to tone with the fabric. The orange lilies (2) and wild tansy (3) provided both a contrast of form and the precise colourings I needed to create a rich and vibrant design. To retain the impact of the colour, restraint in the use of foliage and other plant materials was necessary. Cypress (4) and *Helleborus orientalis* (5) foliage, together with a few sprigs of glycerined alchemilla (6) provided the necessary link with the hessian-covered base.

Figurines in preserved flower arrangements

All flower arrangers love to use figurines, either as containers or just as accessories. Unfortunately, old figurines are becoming increasingly difficult to find, and once found are increasingly difficult to afford. There are reproduction figurines in the shops, but many of the inexpensive ones have plain brown or white surfaces, colours which do little to inspire the arranger interested in creating an arrangement in which plant materials and container are in harmony. Even white figurines are often too ultra-white to use with the creamy white colourings of many preserved flowers. But if you paint one of these figurines in the way described on page 36, you can have at a low cost a figurine which harmonizes with either antique or modern furnishings, according to the paint colours you choose and the way you decide to apply the paint.

A figurine creates movement and interest in an arrangement, but if it is used as an accessory rather than a container it is important that it should be an integral part of the finished arrangement. To see what I mean, compare plate 24 with fig. 5. While in fig. 5 the figurine simply stands at the side of the flower arrangement, in plate 24 it is incorporated into the design.

Bases for preserved arrangements

With fresh flower arrangements a base is often necessary to protect furniture from water stains. This is obviously not a hazard with a preserved flower arrangement, but a base might still be useful. If the plant materials are arranged in a dish or tin which is not intended to be visible in the completed arrangement, a suitable base chosen to complement the arrangement both in style and colour will often enhance the display. Again, when an accessory such as a figurine is used, a suitable base will usually be necessary to unite the arrangement. And a pedestal-type arrangement will often appear more balanced if a base is used. It is very important, however, that a base should always be scaled to the correct size, not too big and not too small—although I think arrangers tend to 'over-base'

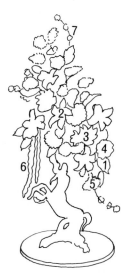

Plate 25 I created this arrangement on a dull winter's day, hoping to give a feeling of warm summer sunshine. The line of the container suggested the shape for my arrangement, for which I used beech foliage (1), day lilies (2), dahlias (3), African Marigolds (4) and yellow statice (5), with pendant tassels of love-lies-bleeding (6). The curious twisting stems of ballota calyces (7) give movement to the arrangement. Details for making the base for this arrangement are shown in fig. 6.

rather than 'under-base'. The base for an arrangement should, like the container, be incorporated into the design of the arrangement. Whether man-made or natural, it should harmonize with the arrangement in shape, size, material and colour. For example, velvet would not make an ideal base for an arrangement in which fungi, ferns and heather were used; natural wood or slate would be a far more suitable choice. A particular colour or shade used in an arrangement can be accentuated by the introduction of a matching or toning shade of colour used for the base.

Designing and making bases can be as interesting and rewarding as preserving and arranging the plant materials. Below are directions for making the three types of bases which I use most often for my own arrangements.

Base 1

I devised the base shown in fig. 6 because I invariably found that however many bases I had I never seemed to have the exact colour for each new arrangement that I designed. So I made a basic cardboard shape and edged it with upholstery braid of a neutral colour. I am now able to make inserts which can easily be changed to suit the colouring of each individual arrangement.

For the base shape cut a circle or an oval from a strong, rigid piece of cardboard (see overleaf). Artists' board from an art shop is ideal. To make the edging, cut a strip of cardboard long enough to go round the base shape and approximately 20 mm ($\frac{3}{4}$ in) wide, just deep enough to form a recess on the base to take the inserts. Glue the edging round the base (fig. 6a) and cover the outside with braid of the appropriate width (fig. 6b). Cut more cardboard shapes to fit inside the edging for the inserts (fig. 6c). These inserts can if you like be cut from thinner card and covered with fabric as described below for base 3. Alternatively, they can be cut from coloured cardboard, which does not need covering.

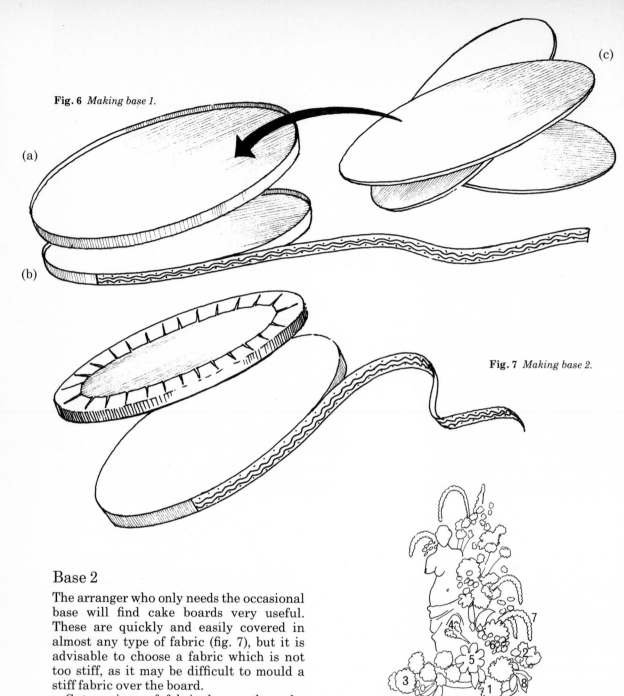

Fig. 6 *Making base 1.*

(a)

(b)

(c)

Fig. 7 *Making base 2.*

Base 2

The arranger who only needs the occasional base will find cake boards very useful. These are quickly and easily covered in almost any type of fabric (fig. 7), but it is advisable to choose a fabric which is not too stiff, as it may be difficult to mould a stiff fabric over the board.

Cut a piece of fabric larger than the board, to allow for turning over. Cut notches round the edge—make sure the notches are not so deep they will show at the edge of the finished board. Place the board over the back of the fabric, turn over the notched edge and stick it down with glue, sticking a little at a time and keeping the fabric taut. Cover the back with a piece of thin card, to make a neat finish.

Plate 26 Another arrangement created in mid-winter and intended to be reminiscent of a garden of summer flowers. With their flowering seasons slightly overlapping, lilacs (1), rambler roses (2), dahlias (3), lavender (4), tree peonies (5) and the daisy-like flowers of feverfew (6) are arranged with individually wired tassels of love-lies-bleeding (7) and choisya leaves (8). The introduction of foliage was kept to a minimum so as not to weaken the impact of the colour. The arrangement is placed on the base shown in fig. 7.

42

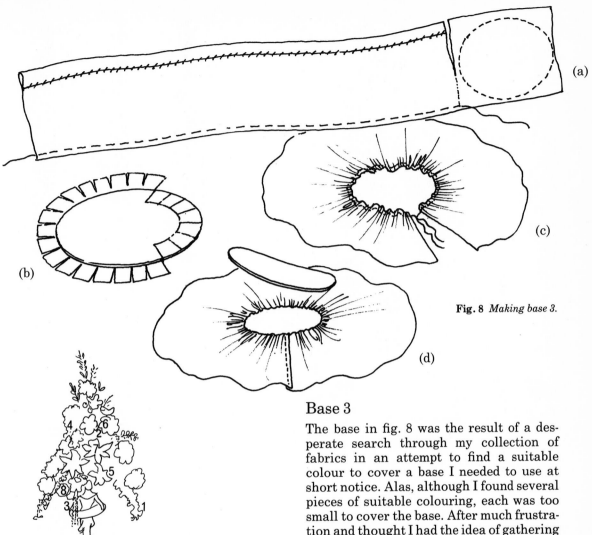

(a)

(b)

(c)

(d)

Fig. 8 *Making base 3.*

Plate 27 A complete contrast to the arrangement in plate 26, this arrangement was intended to create a subdued effect, in harmony with the colouring of the fabric. I chose a spelter figurine as the container for the arrangement. The background of escallonia (1) and aucuba (2) foliage and the catkins of *Garrya elliptica* (3) echo the colouring of the figurine, carrying it through the arrangement. Autumn-gathered hydrangeas (4), statice (5) and honesty seed disc fun flowers (6) in shades of magenta, cerise and mauve are lightened by the introduction of rather faded yellow lilies (7) and tree peonies (8)—another occasion when aged preserved flowers were useful in helping to achieve an effect. I designed the base (see fig. 8) especially to help create a feeling of Victorian elegance in keeping with the figurine.

Base 3

The base in fig. 8 was the result of a desperate search through my collection of fabrics in an attempt to find a suitable colour to cover a base I needed to use at short notice. Alas, although I found several pieces of suitable colouring, each was too small to cover the base. After much frustration and thought I had the idea of gathering a long piece of straight fabric and fixing it round a small central oval shape. I was able to get my base made on time—and using less than 125 mm (5 in) of 120 cm (48 in) wide fabric. It is worth noting that, although this would not be a suitable base for every arrangement, from the point of view of economy, it is possible to get two bases of this type from a 250 mm (10 in) strip of fabric. The amount of gathering varies, depending on the width of the fabric used.

Cut a piece of fabric about 125×180 mm (5×7 in) from the end of your fabric strip. Gather the remaining length of fabric along one long edge. Turn in and stick or stitch a narrow hem on the opposite edge (fig. 8a).

Trim the spare end of fabric to a round or oval shape and cut notches round the edge. Cut from a piece of cardboard a shape which is slightly smaller than your end of fabric. Place the cardboard shape over the back of the fabric, turn the notched edge of the fabric over and stick it down on the cardboard (fig. 8b). Pull up the gathered edge of the long strip of fabric (fig. 8c). Join the two ends and stick the oval shape in position (fig. 8d). Stick a piece of thin card over the back of the central shape, for a neat finish.

Assembling an arrangement

There seem to be endless misconceptions about the arranging of preserved plant materials. The fact is that having collected and preserved your plant materials and given them any of the special treatments suggested, you can then arrange them exactly as you would fresh plant materials. The only special point to remember is that special care should be taken in handling desiccant-preserved flowers and leaves, as some are inclined to be rather fragile.

There is one area in which the arranger of preserved flowers is at a distinct disadvantage. Flowers are often preserved and stored for several months before being used in an arrangement. This means that if when you come to do your arrangement you find you need just one more flower and it is not possible to pop out into the garden to pick one, you will either have to make do, or wait until the flowering season comes round again. It is advisable always to bear this in mind, and to try to plan your arrangement as you preserve your plant materials. If in doubt, preserve one or two extra flowers or leaves.

Before beginning to assemble your preplanned arrangement, check the following points to make quite sure that you have everything ready and prepared.

1 Make sure that you have sufficient flowers, foliage, and any other plant materials that you wish to incorporate.
2 Check for any crystals which may still be hidden between the petals of desiccant-preserved flowers. A firm tap on the stem will dislodge these. Failure to remove all crystals could result in an embarrassing shower from your arrangement every time the container is moved or a flower is touched by an unconvinced guest.
3 Unless your arrangement is to be displayed under perfectly dry conditions, spray large-petalled flowers as soon as they are removed from the storage tin (see page 150).
4 Stand the flowers ready for use in a jar of flower foam, do *not* leave them in a heap on the table.
5 If newly-glycerined evergreen foliage is being used, rub the leaves with oil (see page 156). A little oil will also liven up evergreen foliage which has been stored for some time.
6 Prepare the flower foam for your container (see page 30).
7 Have ready wires and binding wire to enable stems to be lengthened if necessary; also binding tape to cover wire stems (see pages 18 and 23).
8 It is advisable to invest in a pair of special floral art scissors for cutting wires. These are made with a special part of the blade for cutting wires without damage to the main scissor blades.

Now you are ready to make your arrangement. Of course, you will arrange your materials in the way that is pleasing to you, but if you are not familiar with flower arranging you may find the step by step diagrams in fig. 9 a useful guide to the basic principles.

First, position your spiky outline material —cut the stems to varying lengths (fig. 9a).

Then arrange the bold, important flowers (fig. 9b), positioning the smaller ones towards the top.

Finally, fill in with plant materials that in size and type are intermediate between the spiky outline materials and the solid materials (fig. 9c).

Some guidelines to help you create the basic shape of your arrangement can be found in fig. 11.

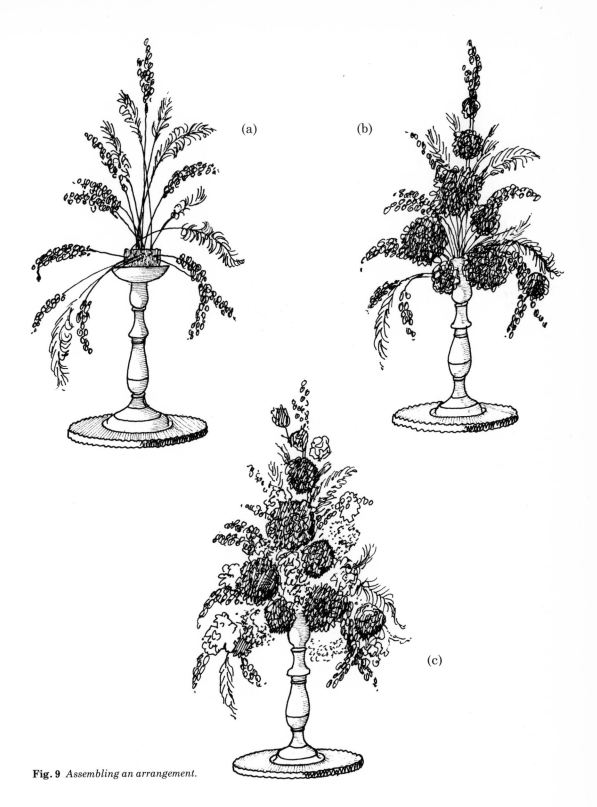

(a)

(b)

(c)

Fig. 9 *Assembling an arrangement.*

Arrangements in their settings

The setting should determine the colour, style and mood of an arrangement. In his or her own home the arranger's personal taste is usually reflected in the décor of each room, which in turn creates the setting for a suitable type of arrangement. For example, a formal room decorated in the style of an earlier period will be enhanced by a graceful arrangement in a harmonious colour scheme, using elegant flowers in a well chosen container. In complete contrast, a modern room usually commands bold plant forms in a well balanced line arrangement (for an example of this see fig. 10). In this type of arrangement the emphasis will often be on using plant forms for their interesting textures rather than for pretty colouring, and containers will often be bolder and more dominant.

Preserved plant materials adapt so well to the role of becoming an integral part of the décor. We can have flowers of every season available when we design our arrangements; and they can be used to create long-lasting colour features incorporating selected furnishing colours.

Each of the arrangements illustrated in plates 7, 24, 27, 28, 29, 30 and 31 was planned to harmonize with a particular fabric, and incorporate plant materials which were carefully chosen for their colour value. If you compare these arrangements with each other you will see how different fabrics can provide inspiration for arrangements which harmonize with the furnishing colour schemes of individual rooms.

Your favourite watercolour or oil painting can also offer a challenge; the effect of a preserved arrangement which picks up the colourings in your picture can often be very rewarding, drawing attention to both picture and arrangement.

A preserved arrangement can be used as a feature of concentrated colour in a room in the same way as a lamp or a cushion is used to accentuate colour.

Plate 28 The firm texture of rudbeckia flowers, with their rich colourings, makes them ideal for preserving. The base covered with dark brown velvet plays a major role in this arrangement, as its colour highlights the rudbeckia centres and accentuates the golden colour of their petals. Individually wired flowers from a spray of florists' carnations (2), and golden rod flowers (3) blend well with the golden theme. The brown foliage is from the shrubs escallonia (4) and viburnum (5). *Hypericum elatum* berries (6), gathered from the garden in January (when they had become naturally dried hollow shells), were varnished to give added sparkle.

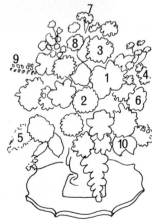

Plate 29 The fabric covers of my chairs inspired this arrangement, and when it was finished it was incorporated into the room as part of the furnishings. Although the flowers I used are not exactly the ones on the fabric, they do create a harmonious effect—and they illustrate how useful a collection of flowers preserved at different seasons can be. The flowers are peonies (1), dahlias (2), hydrangeas (3), feverfew (4), lilacs (5), roses (6), statice (7), tulips (8). I also used mahonia berries (9). Desiccant-preserved leaves of the common whitebeam (10) provided foliage of the ideal colour.

50

Fig. 10 *Bold plant materials placed to form a well balanced line arrangement in a modern room setting— a complete contrast to the arrangement in plate 29.*

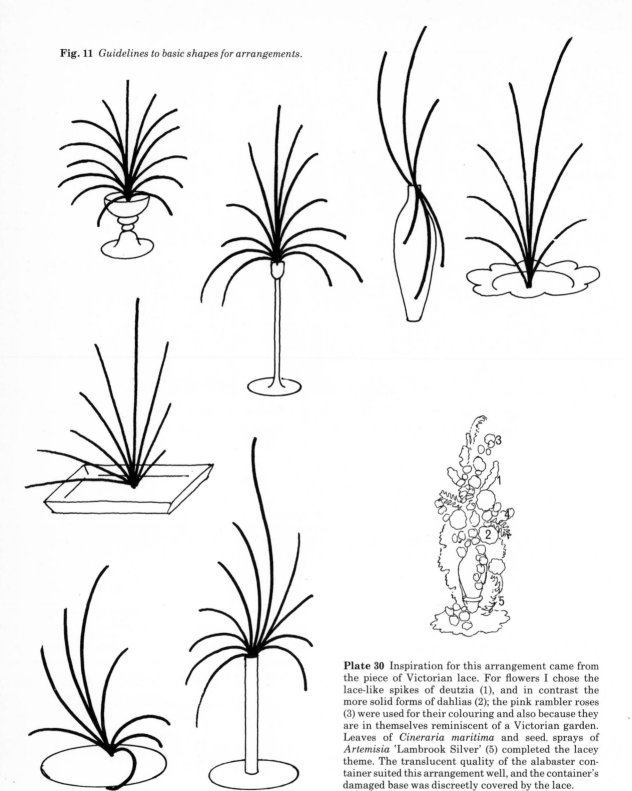

Fig. 11 *Guidelines to basic shapes for arrangements.*

Plate 30 Inspiration for this arrangement came from the piece of Victorian lace. For flowers I chose the lace-like spikes of deutzia (1), and in contrast the more solid forms of dahlias (2); the pink rambler roses (3) were used for their colouring and also because they are in themselves reminiscent of a Victorian garden. Leaves of *Cineraria maritima* and seed. sprays of *Artemisia* 'Lambrook Silver' (5) completed the lacey theme. The translucent quality of the alabaster container suited this arrangement well, and the container's damaged base was discreetly covered by the lace.

The effects of lighting

Without light we would not be able to appreciate and enjoy colour; and it is only successfully making use of the right type of light that the arranger of preserved flowers can produce outstanding and lasting effects with colour. Used well, light can play a major role in presenting preserved arrangements which are visually as bright and attractive as their fresh counterparts. But the wrong kind of light can produce quite disastrous effects on preserved flowers.

Daylight

A preserved arrangement is often positioned on a window sill, in the firm belief that it will show up well against the light. This is a sad misapprehension. Far from enhancing the colours of the flowers, strong, direct ultra-violet rays of sunlight will in fact make many colours appear dull and faded. Even worse, arrangements situated in such a position will in a relatively short time lose most of their colour. The result will be a typically dried-looking arrangement, something which we have spent a considerable amount of time during the various stages of preserving and arranging trying to avoid.

The arranger should note that fading does not occur only when arrangements are placed in a south-facing window. Direct light from other aspects will cause a similar degree of fading.

Artificial light

Tungsten lighting (the light given by an ordinary electric light bulb) is far more flattering to preserved flowers than daylight. It actually enhances all the colours of the flowers, making them appear richer and more luminous. This is particularly apparent with shades of dark red, for example the peonies in plate 31. In fact the ideal setting for an arrangement is an alcove lit by tungsten lighting which can be switched on at any time to create a special effect. It is worth remembering that the warmth of the light would cause fresh flowers in such a position to wilt in a relatively short time, but the warmth will help to keep preserved flowers in perfect condition.

Most types of fluorescent lighting have a disastrous visual effect on most colours of preserved flowers, making them appear dull and dingy. The colours most seriously affected are shades of pink and red—pinks tend to look fawn, and reds take on a muddy brownish overtone. Fortunately, fluorescent light is little used in living rooms, but I find the extensive use of this lighting in public meeting rooms very frustrating. Unless it is offset by adequate additional tungsten spotlighting, fluorescent lighting makes it impossible to show the effectiveness of colour and colour harmony in a preserved flower arrangement.

Plate 31 Featuring six red peonies preserved at various stages of opening, from a bud through to the fully developed flower—from which I have pulled a few petals to reveal the yellow centres. Small red tree peonies were the only other flowers used. The silver leaves of the echinops are used with their undersides uppermost; the rich dark leaves are aucuba. A few sprays of *Stachys lanata* calyces add height and movement to the arrangement. The colour of the velvet-covered base creates a close harmony between arrangement and furnishing fabric. This fabric is too bold and striking to consider using with it an arrangement of delicate and fussy plant materials.

3 The decorative use of driftwood and cones

Driftwood

A book on flower arranging is never really complete without the introduction of wood. I get an enormous amount of pleasure from natural pieces of wood, or driftwood. To the novice this may seem a misleading description for my pieces of wood, when I tell you that most of them were collected from woodlands and forests, and not as you might expect from the seashore. However, according to the National Association of Flower Arranging Societies (NAFAS) rules, if a class in a show stipulates 'An arrangement of driftwood', arrangers are free to use any type of natural wood.

Flower arrangers usually have their own individual approach to the use of wood in arrangements, and it is certainly not for me to say how it should or should not be used, but instead I would like to tell you a little about the wood I use and where I find it. I have also designed arrangements based on my own special way of combining wood with other plant materials, which may be of interest to any arranger who never really knows what to do with an interesting piece of driftwood when he or she finds it.

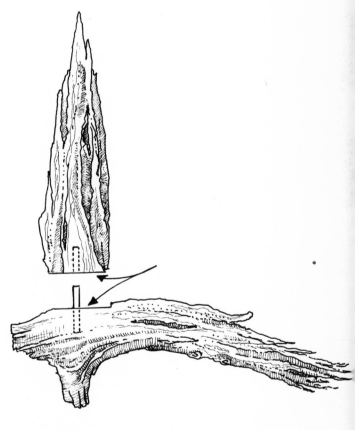

Plate 32 Two interesting pieces of driftwood fixed together as shown in fig. 12 create the basis for a woodland setting in which wild ivy and heather appear to be growing rather than arranged around and through the hollowed yew wood. Flowers of *Helleborus orientalis* are very much in keeping with this type of arrangement and their colouring harmonizes with the heather. Naturally dried emerald green fern moss, which is characteristic of a woodland habitat, hides the Plasticine that holds the plant materials. No! I did not find the wood with the bracket fungi already attached. I glued them into position with clear quick-drying contact adhesive to give a feeling of natural growth. These bracket fungi were an unexpected discovery which gave me particular pleasure. After searching old tree stumps in vain for several seasons, I had given up hope of finding any really good ones. Then I made a trip to the woods in early spring to collect leaves without even a thought of fungi, and there, almost hidden by the undergrowth, were these colourful bracket fungi.

Fig. 12 *The two pieces of wood used in the arrangement in plate 32 are pegged together. The faces of the two pieces are scraped flat, a hole is drilled in each piece, one end of the peg (a piece of wooden dowelling) is inserted in each hole and the two pieces are pulled together.*

The sources from which interesting pieces of driftwood can be collected will largely depend on the area in which you live. I am lucky enough to have wooded areas within walking distance and the New Forest only a short drive away, and these are of course my main hunting grounds. My chances of finding sea-washed driftwood are reserved for holidays or day trips, usually taken during the summer months. For the arranger living in a coastal area, a walk along the beach after a winter storm offers great possibilities.

Maybe you have discovered a really old, interesting-looking piece of forest wood, for instance part of an uprooted tree stump that has lain on the forest floor for many years partly overgrown by encroaching vegetation and broken away from the main part of the stump by the natural process of decay. This is the habitat in which many of my most treasured pieces were found, but it is only by foraging (old clothes are essential), and prodding and poking the piece that you will discover whether or not it is too rotten to be of any use. If the prodding reveals only partial rotting with a substantial proportion of hardwood left, it is quite possible that you have found a piece suitable to clean and develop for an interesting arrangement. Old yew stumps are particularly worth exploring.

An old kitchen knife or a screwdriver is usually the only tool needed to clean up a piece of driftwood and remove any rotten parts. One word of warning: keep your treasured pieces of driftwood in a safe place. I know of many a piece that has ended up not in an arrangement but, sadly, as ashes in the fire grate or on the bonfire.

With driftwood, unlike other plant materials, it is not usually possible just to walk out and find a piece of the exact size and shape for a particular arrangement or an idea that you happen to have in mind. For this reason I usually find that my arrangement starts with the driftwood, and the inspiration for the plant materials to use with it and the style of arrangement usually come from its form, colouring or texture.

My favourite natural driftwood resembles in shape the larger formations of old dead tree stumps that it was originally part of (see plate 33). With this in mind, my preference is to use plant materials which are in harmony with a natural woodland habitat. Good examples of such plant materials are ivy leaves, ferns, bracken, catkins, moss, heather, hellebores and daisies.

In complete contrast are pieces of driftwood like the one shown in plate 34. When cleaned this piece had a smooth appearance, and although it may look painted, I have actually only brushed it over with a clear varnish to emphasize the natural rich, dark colouring of the wood and to increase its durability (it was inclined to be rather brittle). Such a piece is suitable for use in a more formal arrangement, with flowers such as dahlias, or the lilies shown here.

Plate 33 Part of an old fallen tree stump provides ready-made holes and hollows in which lumps of Plasticine, modelling clay or floral clay can be embedded to take preserved plant materials. I have arranged groups of wild heather and bracken ferns in an attempt to re-create a natural woodland setting. Tiny fungi peep out from a moss-covered hollow to give added interest to the arrangement.

Plate 34 In this arrangement just six yellow lilies are shown to advantage against the dark colour of the wood and the almost black glycerined aucuba leaves.

Cones

Readers of my previous books will already have discovered that cones hold a great fascination for me, and wherever I go at home or abroad I just cannot resist the temptation to forage under any conifer I see to gather just a few more to add to my collection. The shape and texture of cones make them so unlike any other plant material, they provide such a useful contrast in an arrangement and their almost indestructible nature makes it possible to use them over and over again, year after year.

Cones of all sizes can be wired to provide interesting flower-like forms for arrangements. Use a fairly thick florists' wire — about a 20-gauge is suitable for average-sized cones. Naturally, a very much finer wire will be used for miniature cones, such as the ones in plate 41. For really large cones two wires can be used together for greater strength.

Bend the wire in half and thread it between the bottom two rows of scales (fig. 14a). Pull the wire taut and it will become embedded between the cone scales. Twist the two ends tightly together and then twist them round the little nodule of stem; continue twisting the ends round each other to form a stem (fig. 14b).

Some cones or part cones, such as the cedar cone centres shown in plate 54, because of their formation cannot be wired. A cone of this type can simply be glued into the top of a strong hollow stem (fig. 14c).

Either type of stem can be bound in the way shown for binding flowers on page 23.

(b)

Fig. 14 *Making stems for cones.*

(a)

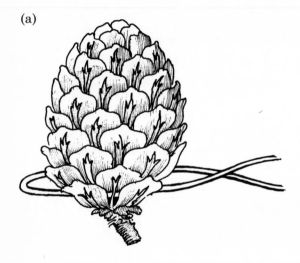

(c)

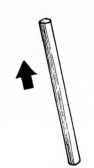

Making plaques with cones

Because of their tough, woody structure, cones do not need the protection of glass, so they are an ideal choice for decorative open plaques. Pine cones are probably the most common and the easiest to collect, and for making the fun flowers shown in plate 58 I found them ideal, but the enthusiastic and observant collector can discover many other cone-bearing trees whose decorative cones will make more interesting plaques (see plates 36 and 37).

Plate 35 Here the flower-like forms of stone pine cones blend with their basket container both in colour and texture. They are arranged against a background of *Eleagnus x ebbingei* foliage. Spiky corn stalks and black yucca seedpods provide contrast of shape.

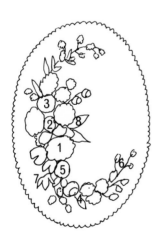

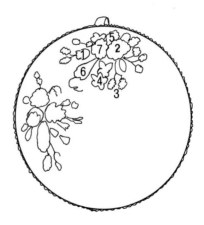

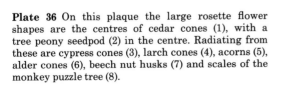

Plate 36 On this plaque the large rosette flower shapes are the centres of cedar cones (1), with a tree peony seedpod (2) in the centre. Radiating from these are cypress cones (3), larch cones (4), acorns (5), alder cones (6), beech nut husks (7) and scales of the monkey puzzle tree (8).

Plate 37 Four individual placements of cones and seedpods make up this design which is mounted on a hessian background. The texture of hessian is ideal to use with this type of plant material—poppy seedpods (1), larch cones (2), alder cones (3), beech nuts (4), cypress cones (5), lily seedpods (6), pine cones (7).

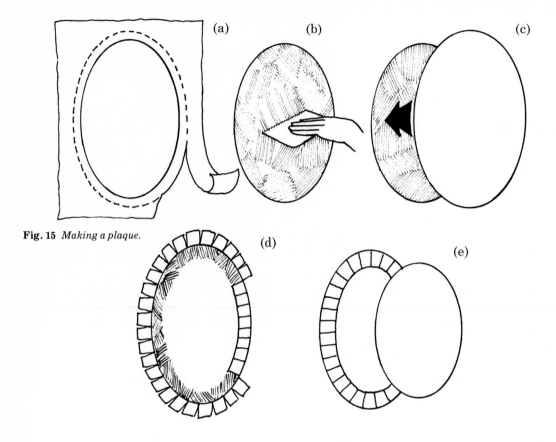

Fig. 15 *Making a plaque.*

(a) (b) (c) (d) (e)

To make a plaque you will need, apart from your plant materials, the following equipment.:

Stiff cardboard or hardboard
Fabric
PVA or latex glue
A picture hook (if you intend to hang your plaque)
Clear contact adhesive

Decide what shape you want for your mount. I find round and oval shapes more attractive for plaques than squares and oblongs with their hard, pointed corners. Cut the mount shape out of cardboard or hardboard. Then cut a fabric shape about 25 mm (1 in) larger all round than the mount (fig. 15a). Cover one side of the mount with a thin coat of latex glue (fig. 15b). Be careful to spread the glue evenly all over the back—

if places are left uncovered you will later find bubbles appearing in the fabric. Spread the fabric over the glued surface, smoothing it as you work but being careful not to stretch it (fig. 15c). Turn your plaque over and spread a thin band of glue about 25 mm (1 in) wide round the edge of the mount. Cut v-shaped notches out of the edge of the fabric so that it will lie evenly, then turn the fabric edge over on to the glued area and smooth it down (fig. 15d). To give the back of the plaque a neat finish, glue on a piece of fabric, thin card or paper cut 12 mm ($\frac{1}{2}$ in) smaller all round than the mount (fig. 15e). If you like, attach a picture hook for hanging.

Arrange your plant materials on the plaque. When you are satisfied with your arrangement, glue the materials in place, using a contact adhesive.

4 Miniature and petite designs

Styles, fashions and ideas change each year, but one thing that never changes is the fascination with tiny things, among them tiny flower arrangements. At a national or local exhibition of flower arrangements or even a village flower show, the enthusiasm for miniature arrangements is always keen among both exhibitors and viewers.

Many readers will, I am sure, only be interested in creating small arrangements for their own homes or as gifts for friends. However, arrangers wishing to compete in the appropriate classes of shows or flower arrangement societies which are judged by NAFAS rules should carefully observe the required measurements. The NAFAS definitions booklet divides small arrangements into two groups: 'A miniature design'—an exhibit not more than 102 mm (4 in) overall; and 'A petite design'—an exhibit more than 102 mm (4 in) and less than 229 mm (9 in) overall.

It is often thought that to be able to create miniature arrangements it is necessary to grow miniature flowers, but this is not at all the case when working with preserved flowers. If I had more time to devote to gardening I am sure I would concentrate on growing plants especially for miniature work, as I find it so fascinating. However, I am sure there are many people who, like myself, have just an average-sized garden with a selection of ordinary garden plants from which they would like to work in miniature. And in fact I designed and made all the arrangements in this section from wild plant materials and quite common garden flowers and leaves which I gathered from my own garden. If you study my miniature arrangements you will discover that to find materials you just need to look at your garden and the countryside through different eyes, with miniature work in mind.

The most important thing with a miniature or petite arrangement is that all the plant materials and the container should be on the same scale. After all, a miniature arrangement is only a scaled-down version of a large arrangement. For example, in the miniature arrangement in plate 39 individual florets of saxifrage take the place of the lilies of a large arrangement, and a spiky blade from a clump of garden pinks is used instead of an iris leaf. In fig. 16 you will see an example of an unbalanced arrangement, where the plant materials are the wrong size for the container. Plate 40 shows the same container arranged with materials of an appropriate size.

Plant materials for miniature arrangements

When miniature arrangements are created with fresh flowers, it is of course essential that each flower should have a sufficiently long stem to enable it to be inserted into water-retaining material. When working with preserved plant materials we have much more scope; for example, a single head of lilac will provide dozens of tiny florets, each of which, wired individually, will become a miniature flower. The large, flat, plate-like heads of achillea can be divided in the same way—I used tiny segments of an achillea head in the walnut shell arrangement in plate 40.

It is often possible to divide achillea heads in such a way that each segment has a long enough stem without wiring. And achillea stems are strong enough to support the florets after preserving. Some other flowers, such as delphiniums, have florets with firm, wiry stems that are reasonably

Plate 38 This interestingly-shaped lump of wood is exactly as I found it. Although it measures only 65 mm (2$\frac{1}{2}$ in) high by 50 mm (2 in) wide, it resembles many large stumps which I have looked at longingly in the forest but which proved too large and heavy to take home. After carefully studying my miniature log I decided that the best way to incorporate plant material was to make two simple placements of wild heather, wild achillea and tiny fern fronds taken from wild bracken. The plant materials are held in place by modelling clay. 102 × 102 × 75 mm (4 × 4 × 3 in).

Plate 39 A little rusty metal dish took on a new lease of life after I gave it a coat of black paint. Five white Mossy Saxifrage flowers, looking rather like tiny lilies, were the only flowers needed to create this miniature. I have arranged them with little rosettes of their own foliage together with three spiky leaves from a clump of garden pinks. The plant materials are held in place by a small piece of flower foam glued to the container. 102 × 65 × 65 mm (4 × 2$\frac{1}{2}$ × 2$\frac{1}{2}$ in).

Plate 40 Two empty halves of a walnut shell found under my walnut tree at the end of the winter needed nothing more than a blob of glue to make them into this miniature container. A small chunk of flower foam glued inside holds the arrangement of wall ferns, maidenhair spleenwort, montbretia buds, tiny sprigs taken from a large flat head of *Achillea filipendulina* and the woody seedheads of rhododendron. 75 × 90 × 50 mm (3 × 3½ × 2 in).

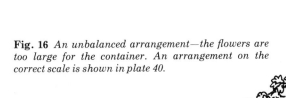

Fig. 16 An unbalanced arrangement—the flowers are too large for the container. An arrangement on the correct scale is shown in plate 40.

long and strong enough when preserved to use without wiring. However, it is generally advisable to wire tiny flowers. The little stems are usually so slender that they can easily be broken while an arrangement is being made up. The size of wire to use depends entirely on the size and weight of the flower, and some experimenting will be necessary. For really tiny, lightweight flowers fine silver florists' wires are best (see fig. 17 on page 70).

Flowers should be wired before preserving. Just push the wire down through the middle of the flower and the stem (fig. 17a). If it is necessary to lengthen a stem, this is done after preserving, in exactly the same way as for larger flowers (see page 23).

For all but the very nimble-fingered, wiring really tiny flowers, such as the saxifrage flowers shown in plate 39, is just too tricky. The easiest solution to this problem is to stick each preserved flower by its stem to a length of silver wire (fig. 17b).

I find that both the wire stems and the natural stems of miniature flowers are far too fiddly to bind with tape, and so I rely on ensuring that each stem is covered by another flower or leaf (fig. 17c).

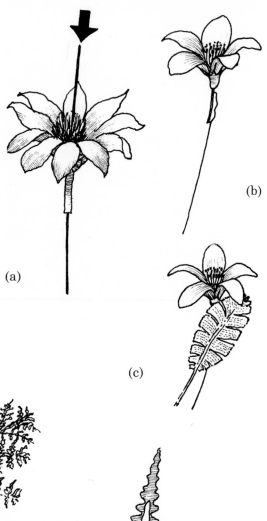

Fig. 17 *Extending the stems of tiny flowers.*

(a)

(b)

(c)

Fig. 18a *An individual frond taken from a fern becomes a miniature fern.*

Just as large preserved arrangements need foliage, so do miniature ones. For the arrangement in plate 40 I used tiny fronds, only 40 mm (1½ in) long, of the wall fern maidenhair spleenwort. These were on exactly the right scale for this tiny arrangement. But do not worry if such dainty ferns are not within your reach; in fig. 18a you will see how a large frond of the common bracken fern can be divided to give an adequate supply of miniature ferns, in varying sizes and lengths, for many arrangements. Cut off each tiny segment from its main stem and glue a length of florists' silver wire to the back to provide a false stem. Some of these miniature ferns have been used in the arrangement in plate 41.

Plate 41 A fragment of driftwood makes an interesting textured base for a group of tiny larch cones, wild poppy seedheads, wild ivy leaves and fern fronds. The ivy leaves were collected during the winter. At this time of year many of the mature leaves have this beautiful veining, which I think is as attractive as that of any cultivated ivy. A tiny twig of contorted hazel gives the necessary height and balance to this arrangement. Modelling clay holds the plant materials. 102 × 102 × 70 mm (4 × 4 × 2¾ in).

Plate 42 Scent bottles are often much too attractive to throw away. This elegant Worth glass bottle at once made me think of glycerine-preserved escallonia leaves, which turn almost black after preserving but retain their glossy surfaces. The little bottle, only 50 mm (2 in) high, seemed to be made especially for them. I chose cerise flowers to provide a marked contrast to the black. Any tiny cerise flowers or florets would be suitable, but I happened to have buds of the common *Fuchsia magellanica* and tiny cornflowers—tiny because they were picked at the end of their flowering season. A small lump of Plasticine moulded over the neck of the bottle holds the plant materials. $102 \times 50 \times 40$ mm ($4 \times 2 \times 1\frac{1}{2}$ in).

A supply of bolder, more solid-looking leaves can be achieved by removing leaves from sprays of foliage and glueing each one to a length of florists' silver wire (fig. 18b). Plate 43 shows escallonia leaves used in this way.

A blob of glue squeezed on the base of the wire or natural stem before it is inserted into flower foam will hold your flowers and leaves firmly in position and help to keep your arrangement intact if it is to be transported to an exhibition.

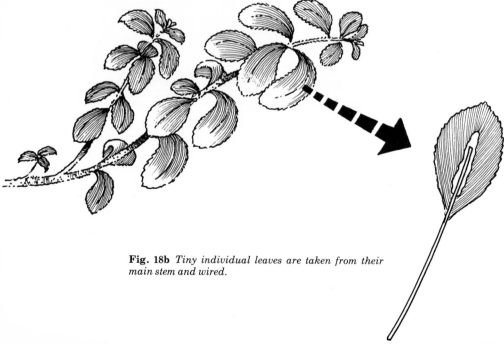

Fig. 18b *Tiny individual leaves are taken from their main stem and wired.*

Containers for miniature and petite arrangements

When you turn the pages of this section of my book you will see that I have used many different plant materials for miniature and petite arrangements, and as many different types of containers and bases. I always spend quite a lot of time trying plant materials with containers before I actually create an arrangement. This is great fun, and you gradually become aware of which container looks right with which plant material. This experimenting is of course much easier with miniature than with full-size arrangements, as half a dozen containers and a selection of little flowers together with other bits and pieces of plant materials take up so little room they can conveniently be spread out on the kitchen table or some other suitable work top. When working on miniatures I practically always start with the container and link the plant materials to the container. I find the challenge very rewarding.

Sometimes it is necessary to concentrate on colouring: see, for example, the arrangement illustrated in plate 43. The orange shades of the flowers appeared to be the perfect complement to the miniature copper jug. The slender black glass scent bottle shown in plate 42 seemed to need bold colourings to create an overall balance, and the tiny, almost black, glycerined leaves of the escallonia provided the necessary link with the container. I also felt that this container demanded a slender line arrangement rather than a mass of flowers. The container so often dictates both the colour and the style of an arrangement.

Plate 43 The rich gold and bronze shades of these miniature zinnias are arranged with sprays of montbretia buds and individual montbretia florets. Copper-coloured leaves help to create a warm harmony between the arrangement and the miniature antique copper jug. A tiny greeny-gold velvet base harmonizes with the centres of the zinnia flowers and the tiny pieces of naturally dried cypress foliage. A small piece of flower foam was wedged into the neck of the jug to take the plant materials. $165 \times 65 \times 65$ mm ($6\frac{1}{2} \times 2\frac{1}{2} \times 2\frac{1}{2}$ in).

Plate 44 A small wine glass filled with tiny pieces of broken windscreen glass makes an ideal container for a petite arrangement. The delightful pink 'Cécile Brunner' roses, which retain their form so well as they open, are great favourites of mine. Here I have arranged them with green and cream variegated leaves preserved from an indoor ivy plant. $150 \times 102 \times 65$ mm $(6 \times 4 \times 2\frac{1}{2}$ in).

Plate 45 For this miniature arrangement I chose a blue and grey theme to complement the tiny grey china pot. Individual florets were taken from a spike of a small-flowered delphinium to provide miniature blue flowers. I took some buds from the spike as well. The silver leaves are from the centre of *Cineraria maritima*. The four spiky leaves are from a clump of garden pinks, and the two silver buds from the shrub *Senecio greyi*. A small piece of flower foam was wedged into the neck of the pot to take the plant materials. $102 \times 50 \times 50$ mm ($4 \times 2 \times 2$ in).

Plate 46 The miniature silver-coloured plate was a junk shop find, very cheap because it is only chromium-plated, not real silver. It makes an ideal base for this arrangement of blue hydrangea florets (1), forget-me-nots (2) and pink florets from an ornamental double cherry tree (3), together with the more unusual cream and green buds and florets of Solomon's Seal (4) and two carefully selected curved stems of the perennial statice (5). Very little foliage was needed—just three feathery leaves from the rockery perennial *Chrysanthemum haradjanii* (6). The plant materials are held by flower foam secured with florists' fixative. $75 \times 65 \times 65$ mm ($3 \times 2\frac{1}{2} \times 2\frac{1}{2}$ in).

Collecting suitable items for putting preserved flowers in or on can be an absorbing and fascinating hobby in itself. Your collection can be as expensive or inexpensive as you choose. A miniature antique curio may be perfect with just the right choice of preserved flowers, but an empty scent bottle with an interesting shape can be equally appropriate. For the enthusiastic collector all types of shops are potential sources of items suitable for miniature containers. Several of the containers I used in the arrangements illustrated were bought in junk shops. If, like me, you are the sort of person who easily gets carried away in such places, it is a good idea to give yourself a price limit.

Apart from man-made items, I collect twigs, pieces of wood and pieces of slate and stone, in fact anything that is interesting in shape, colour or texture. I find shells particularly fascinating. Shells seem to have an affinity with plant materials. Their colours, textures and shapes are often an inspiration to flower arrangers. Some people are lucky enough to be able to collect their own shells, but most of us have to buy them. However, although most of the shells in the shops are imported, they are usually quite inexpensive. Holiday resort souvenir shops make good hunting places, but shells seem to appear in all kinds of shops. Once you begin looking for shells you will undoubtedly discover a great many different shapes (see fig. 20 for some examples). The insides of some of the flatter shells are the most beautiful iridescent colours, which can be taken as the starting point for the colour scheme of an arrangement (see plate 47 on the opposite page).

Plate 47 Shells make ideal containers for flowers, but it seemed best to create an arrangement round rather than in this shell, so as not to hide the shape or the beautiful mother-of-pearl lining. I emphasized the silver, pink, mauve and turquoise shading of the shell by using silver *Cineraria maritima* (1) and acaena (2) leaves, pinky-mauve xeranthemum (3), mauve heather (4) and statice (5), and mahonia berries (6). $140 \times 125 \times 75$ mm ($5\frac{1}{2} \times 5 \times 3$ in).

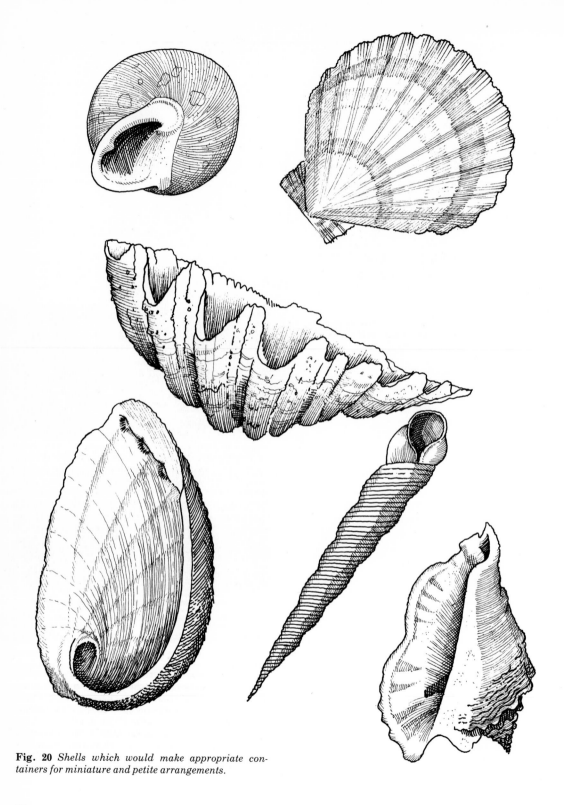

Fig. 20 *Shells which would make appropriate containers for miniature and petite arrangements.*

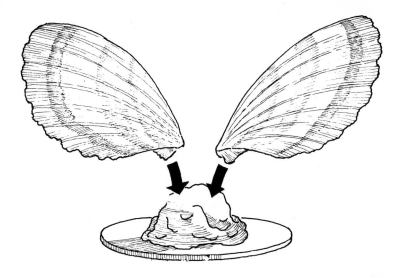

Fig. 21 *Two shells are fixed in a small mound of modelling clay positioned on a cardboard base, in preparation for the arrangement shown in plate 48.*

Plate 48 Another way to use the natural colourings and shape of shells to create an unusual miniature. Here again the shells were the inspiration for both the shape and the colouring of the arrangement. Three tiny faded chrysanthemums provide the ideal colouring, spiky montbretia seedheads have been added for height, and segments taken from a wine-coloured autumn vine leaf make four individual miniature leaves. For details of assembling the shell formation see fig. 21. $95 \times 75 \times 65$ mm ($3\frac{3}{4} \times 3 \times 2\frac{1}{2}$ in).

79

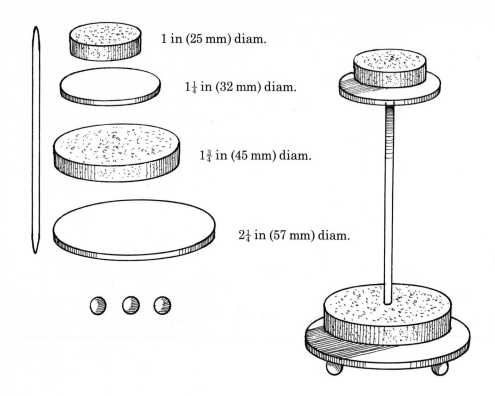

1 in (25 mm) diam.

1¼ in (32 mm) diam.

1¾ in (45 mm) diam.

2¼ in (57 mm) diam.

Fig. 22 *Making a two-tier container for a petite arrangement.*

Making a petite two-tier container

As preserved flowers are very light in weight and of course need no water, containers, especially for miniature and petite arrangements, are very easy to make. The idea for the container shown in fig. 22 came to me while I was looking at a Victorian epergne arranged with fresh flowers.

To make this petite two-tier container you will need the following materials:

  2 round pieces of flower foam, one slightly larger than the other
  2 round pieces of cardboard, one a little bigger than the larger circle of foam, the other a little bigger than the smaller circle of foam
Contact adhesive
3 small beads
A cocktail stick

The most important consideration is getting the proportions just right, to enable you to create a well balanced arrangement. The measurements given on the diagram are those of the container in plate 49, which holds a finished arrangement 150 mm (6 in) high.

To make the base, stick the larger circle of foam to the larger cardboard shape. Stick the beads on for the feet, then push one end of the cocktail stick into the foam. Stick the smaller piece of foam to the smaller piece of cardboard for the top, and push the other end of the cocktail stick through the cardboard into the foam.

Plate 49 Almost any tiny flowers could be used in this two-tiered container. I chose the lovely limey green alchemilla (1), statice in varying shades of pink and mauve (2), fuchsia buds (3) and florets of rambler roses (4). Tiny blades of wild quaking grass (5) give height to the arrangement. 150 × 102 × 102 mm (6 × 4 × 4 in).

Plate 50 A chromium-plated candlestick holds an arrangement of miniature pink roses (1), florets of the rambler rose 'Dorothy Perkins' (2) and little cerise fuchsia flowers (3). Tiny pieces of grey foliage are recessed between the flowers. Spiky pieces of perennial statice (4) and wild artemisia (5) provide a contrast to the more solid forms of the flowers. 229 × 125 × 102 mm (9 × 5 × 4 in).

Fig. 23 *Making a container to fit into the top of a small candlestick.*

(a)

(b)

A small candlecup holder

Even the smallest candlecup holders that can be bought are, I find, too large for tiny candlesticks such as the one used in plate 50. Fortunately, however, a holder can easily be made from a suitably sized bottle or jar top and an ordinary wine bottle cork. If the cork is too large, shave it down with a sharp knife until one end is just the right size to fit firmly and securely into the top of the candlestick. Apply glue to the other end of the cork and attach it to the outside of the bottle top (fig. 23a). Leave the holder overnight to ensure a strong adhesion. Cut a piece of flower foam about twice the depth of the holder and wedge it firmly in place (fig. 23b). The added depth will enable you to insert some plant materials at an angle, to create a downward flow in an arrangement. Fix the holder in the top of your candlestick.

Bases for miniature and petite arrangements

Some miniature and petite arrangements can be greatly enhanced by a suitable base made from or covered in a material chosen to complement the arrangement (see pages 73–86). I must emphasize that 'suitable' is the key word here. You must ensure that the base is appropriate in size. A charming and delicate miniature can be ruined by an overpowering base.

Even with something as small as a miniature, it is important that the base should have a purpose and a sense of belonging to the arrangement. With some arrangements the base actually acts as the container—the arrangement is made directly on the base. Examples are the wood base used in plate 41 and the stone base in plate 51. The other reason for using a base is to create a balance. This was necessary with the shell arrangement in plate 48 where, because of the position of the two shells, all the weight is at the top of the arrangement. For this arrangement I used a simple oval base cut from thin coloured card, to create a visual balance in shape, colour and size. Try different colours and you will soon begin to see which colours are most suitable. Velvet is an ideal material to use for petite arrangements but, unless great care is taken in getting the size exactly right, it may be too heavy for a miniature arrangement. Silky fabrics harmonize particularly well with miniature arrangements, which require only lightweight bases.

Often you will find that an edging will greatly improve a base, although attaching an edging to a tiny base may prove too tedious a job for many people. Again, scale is very important. For example, while a similar type of base made for a full-scale arrangement would probably have a decorative edging of braid, for the miniature base in plate 52 I used silver embroidery cord. Similar gold and silver cords can be bought from needlework shops and crafts shops. Even small cards of parcel cord from the stationer's can be used, provided that they are of a fine enough quality.

This chapter contains just a small selection of my ideas for miniature and petite preserved arrangements. I have included as many different types and styles of arrangements as is possible in the available space, but equally many have had to be left out. Working with preserved flowers in miniature can be very rewarding, and I hope this section of my book will encourage readers who would enjoy working in miniature to explore the possibilities of this aspect of flower arranging.

Plate 51 Collected from a mountainous outcrop of rocks, while we were on holiday in Corfu, this micaschist (a combination of mica and quartz) shines like crystal as it catches the light. A small lump of modelling clay covered with lichen holds in place a lichen-covered branch of wild heather and some tiny white saxifrage flowers. I felt that the subtle beauty of the stone would be overwhelmed if it were combined with colourful plant materials. $102 \times 102 \times 65$ mm ($4 \times 4 \times 2\frac{1}{2}$ in).

Plate 52 Another junk shop discovery, this tiny silver-plated container with its ball and claw feet was an inexpensive buy because although the outside was in good condition the inside was worn away and very tatty. This did not matter to me at all, as I knew the inside would be filled with flowers. The mauve and cerise of the desiccant-preserved hydrangea florets (1) and fuchsia buds (2) harmonize with the everlasting flowers, cerise and mauve statice (3) and pink rhodanthe (4). A few little silver leaves (5) and two tiny seed sprays from the wild artemisia (6) provide the only foliage—more would have destroyed the impact of colour that I wanted to create. I used a cardboard base covered in silky material in a delicate shade of pink and edged with silver embroidery cord. The plant materials are held by flower foam secured with florists' fixative. $75 \times 95 \times 70$ mm ($3 \times 3\frac{3}{4} \times 2\frac{3}{4}$ in).

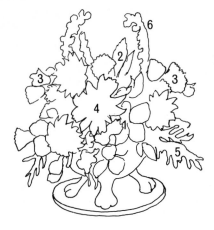

5 Fun flowers

I use the term 'fun flowers' for what are often referred to as contrived flowers—flower-like shapes made from plant materials. Not only are they fun to make, it is fun to search for materials from different plants that will complement each other. Fun flowers should not be confused with artificial flowers made from plastic, silk, glass, feathers or whatever. And although I have seen very good made-up flowers using cardboard discs, buttons and foam shapes as a basis on which to build a flower shape, I prefer to make my flowers entirely from plant materials. The thrill of achieving a successful result sometimes makes me feel as if I had bred my own unique flower! Anyone can be creative and dream up new flowers; you do not have to be clever or talented, but just to develop an ability to look, to see and to experiment. I have concentrated on designing flower-like forms that I feel are easy to construct and yet effective, and I hope readers will be encouraged to have a go at making fun flowers. I am sure you will come to agree that the easiest to make are usually the most effective. It really is just a question of putting together two or more plant parts that in size, shape and form and, most important, colour (unless you intend to paint the finished flower) make an effective and interesting flower. Imported contrived flowers can be bought from garden centres and florists' shops, but the cost is very high when compared to the cost of making your own, which amounts to no more than the price of a tube of clear quick-drying contact adhesive and a few florists' wires.

Naturally, ideas for fun flowers most often come from plants themselves. Sometimes while I am walking round the garden some plant form just happens to catch my eye and inspire me to create a new flower —see, for example, the flower-covered branches in plate 55. Sometimes I hoard plant materials for quite a long time, until suddenly one day I just happen to look at maybe a seedhead while I am making up a preserved arrangement and an idea is sparked off as to how I could use it, or part of it, to construct an interesting flower-like shape.

When putting together parts taken from more than one plant, careful consideration should be given to the appropriateness of combinations of plant forms and textures. For instance, if I had used fir cones instead of doronicum seedheads (picked after their fluffy centres had gone) as centres for the flowers made from honesty seed discs shown in plate 64, the hard, woody texture of the cones would not have complemented the translucent honesty discs so effectively. The result might have been interesting, but it would not have been the delicate flower-like shapes that harmonize with the alabaster container.

I never actually copy any real flowers, but if you analyze my flowers—as I have done long after making them—you will see that without actually being aware of the fact I have made most of them as variations on a basic flower form, for example, a daisy or an arum lily. Although this is not the way I worked, I thought the diagrams in fig. 24 might be helpful to readers who are not familiar with basic flower formations, but may prefer to start with a flower shape in mind and then search for plant materials that will lend themselves to producing a flower based on this shape.

It is most important to consider the sizes of flowers you need for an arrangement, and not only to make a range of different-

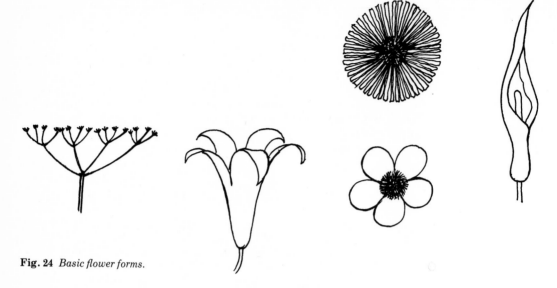

Fig. 24 *Basic flower forms.*

sized flowers from different plant parts but also to make different-sized flowers of the same type. This will create a more interesting and natural-looking arrangement—remember, real flowers are never all the same size! Variation in size is easily achieved—simply select different-sized plant materials for centres and petals.

'Flowers' from cones

The formation of cone scales makes cones ideal as flower centres in which other plant materials can be stuck to form petals. I decided to make a cone-centred fun flower that would harmonize with other plant materials to make an effective arrangement without the addition of any real preserved flowers. The cones I chose for the arrangement illustrated in plate 53 are those of the Japanese larch, which, to me, always look like little wooden roses. In between the lower scales I inserted a circle of naturally dried maple keys which were gathered as soon as they were mature but while they were still green. If maple keys are left on the tree until autumn they lose their colour and are really only interesting if they are bleached.

Plate 53 The red autumn leaves (1) of the maple were an obvious choice of foliage for this arrangement of cone-centred fun flowers (2). Their green maple key petals have a slight reddish tinge whch harmonizes with the tall green and reddish bronze spikes of the wild dock (3). The green and golden fronds of wild bracken (4) contrast with the more solid forms of the fun flowers and the large pine cones (5) at the base of the arrangement. Although this arrangement gives the appearance of being assembled directly on a polished wooden tray, a shallow ceramic container with a block of flower foam in it actually holds the plant materials.

Pampas grass 'flowers'

The tall, stately plumes of fluffy pampas grasses swaying in an autumn breeze remind the flower arranger that they must be cut and dried for winter decoration. But, alas, when picked at this stage they will inevitably shed fluffy bits everywhere. Many arrangers who experience this turn to the often-recommended hair spray treatment, but the real secret is to gather the grasses just as the heads are opening from their sheaths, before they become mature and fluffy. We tend to forget with grasses that the plume is the flowering head of the plant and when fully mature it disintegrates to release its seeds.

Fun flowers based on pampas grass are very simple and economical to make. One large plume of pampas grass is sufficient to make many flowers, and arranged against a background of dark foliage they can look very effective. The arrangement in plate 54 was prepared several months ago and since

Fig. 25 *Small pieces of pampas grass are glued into the valve openings of a poppy seedhead.*

Plate 54 Fun flowers made from cream pampas grass (1) are arranged against a background of dark, almost leathery mahonia leaves (2), together with a few sprays of beech leaves (3) and the individually wired golden leaves of the eleagnus (4). The tiny golden flowers with dark centres are made from box leaves and alder cones (5). Some lily seedheads (6) and three fun flowers made from cedar cones (7) add interest and contrast within the arrangement. The container is an old metal urn which has been painted as described on page 34, to give an antique appearance.

then many friends have remarked on the preserved 'chrysanthemums'. Sometimes I have simply smiled and later felt just a little guilty for not enlightening them, especially as large, fluffy chrysanthemums will not preserve successfully.

To achieve the beautiful silky texture of the fun flowers in plate 54 the pampas grasses should be preserved by the glycerine method (see page 153). Each head is then divided into lots of smaller pieces, which are glued into the valve openings that appear round the top of a mature poppy seedhead (fig. 25). These tiny valves make poppy seedheads perfect centres for fun flowers, as they provide ready-made holders for plant materials. It is important that the poppy seedhead should be mature, because the valves on an immature seedhead will remain tightly closed. You can make flowers of different sizes by using smaller or larger pieces of pampas grass, and because the angle of the valves in relation to the top of the seedhead varies it is possible to have some flowers more fully open than others. There is no need to worry about stems for your flowers, as the poppy seedheads have their own natural stems.

Flower-covered branches

The idea for my flower-covered branches (plate 55) came to me when in late summer I saw the ground under my large clump of acanthus (Bears' Breeches) strewn with white bracts. Immediately I saw them they reminded me of the small varieties of orchids or even magnolia flowers and I felt I must do something interesting with them. It seemed obvious from the formation of these bracts with their stamens attached that they ought to be pushed or threaded on a branch or false stem. As with most flower spikes, the individual florets open a few at a time over quite a long period, which means remembering to collect a few at a time as and when they mature. As each floret matures the bracts and attached stamens become firm and dry to the touch and are forced out by the formation of the seed. I suggest picking or rather pulling these out (fig. 26) as soon as they feel dry, rather than waiting for them to fall, because lying on the ground they soon get damaged and eaten by insects.

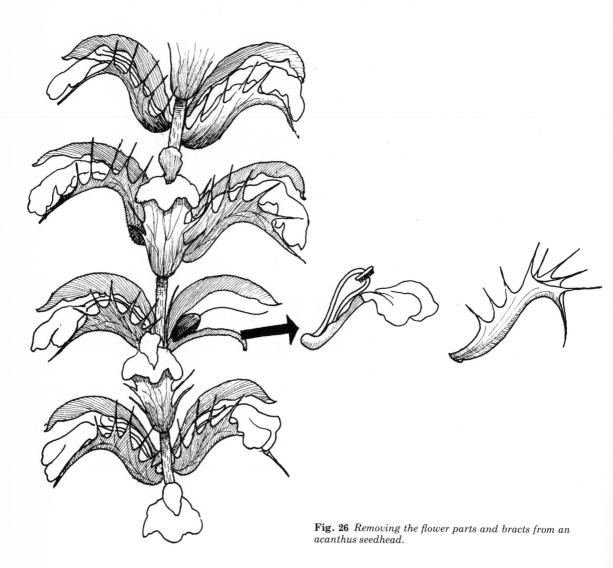

Fig. 26 *Removing the flower parts and bracts from an acanthus seedhead.*

Plate 55 Acanthus bracts are here threaded on a lichen-covered branch, to create a Japanese effect. The branch is anchored with a lump of Plasticine to the inside of an old Britannia metal teapot. The teapot was a gift from an antique dealer who rescued it for me after he had actually thrown it out. Being very damaged it had neither domestic nor antique value, but to the preserved flower arranger items such as this are valuable for their shape. The colouring of this teapot harmonizes particularly well with that of the branch.

Artichoke seedhead 'flowers'

After flowering, the globe artichoke has contained within its seedhead a wealth of material from which interesting fun flowers can be made. At this stage of maturity the fleshy scales become dry and hard, and if the ripe head is pulled apart the beautiful, gleaming, satiny inner surface of the scales appears. When the dead flowering centre is pulled out, a golden hairy seed boss is revealed (fig. 27). The diagrams in figs. 28, 29 and 30 illustrate the making of three different types of fun flowers from artichoke seedheads. The capital letters in these figures and in the directions below refer to the parts marked by those letters in fig. 27.

To make the flower shown in plate 57, choose a wide-open beech nut husk with a small stalk; into its centre glue another beech nut husk which is only half open (fig. 28). To provide your flower with an artificial stem, glue the stalk of the outer beech nut into a hollow plant stalk. Take four of the large, almost woody artichoke bracts (D) and glue these to the outside of the outer beech nut husk. Glue four smaller bracts (C) into the inner beech nut husk. Gather together a small cluster of the hairs from the boss of the artichoke (A) and glue it into position in the centre of the inner nut husk.

For the type of flower shown in plate 58, stick artichoke bracts from the inner rows (B and C) alternately round the back of a rudbeckia seedhead or a similar dark seedhead which will provide a contrast to the pale surface of the artichoke bracts (fig. 29). Make sure that the satiny inner surface of the bracts is kept to the inside of your fun flower—the naturally curved shapes of the bracts will then automatically produce a flower with the petals curving inwards.

Plate 56 When I came to select plant materials to harmonize with my exotic-looking flowers (1), naturally dried magnolia leaves (2), glycerine-preserved cypress foliage (3) and poppy (4) and iris (5) seedheads seemed an ideal choice. Their colours harmonize and they provide contrast in shape and form. The orange candle supplied a link with the orange centres of the flowers, carrying the colour through the arrangement. A plastic dish containing a block of flower foam holds the arrangement; the dish has been placed on a round base covered with an odd piece of fabric left over from making a skirt.

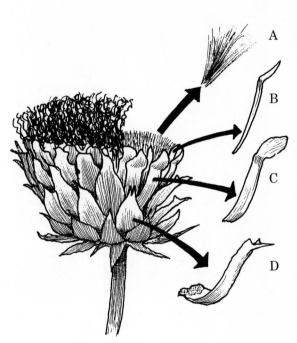

Fig. 27 *A mature artichoke seedhead, showing the variously sized bracts and the hairy boss.*

Plate 57 One of my favourite fun flowers. It can be seen gilded in plate 79 and used in an arrangement in plate 80. Although I cannot relate this to any real flower, I did in fact make it shortly after returning from a holiday in Madeira, and I think with the beautiful orchid and hibiscus flowers still in my mind. (See fig. 28.)

Plate 58 This daisy-type flower could have its petals gilded, but I prefer not to cover the beautiful satiny inner surface of the artichoke bracts, which contrasts so well with the black rudbeckia seedhead centre. (See fig. 29.)

Plate 59 An exotic-looking flower, and yet very simple to make using artichoke seedhead bracts, a pine cone and a Cape Gooseberry calyx. (See fig. 30.) These flowers are used in the arrangement illustrated in plate 56.

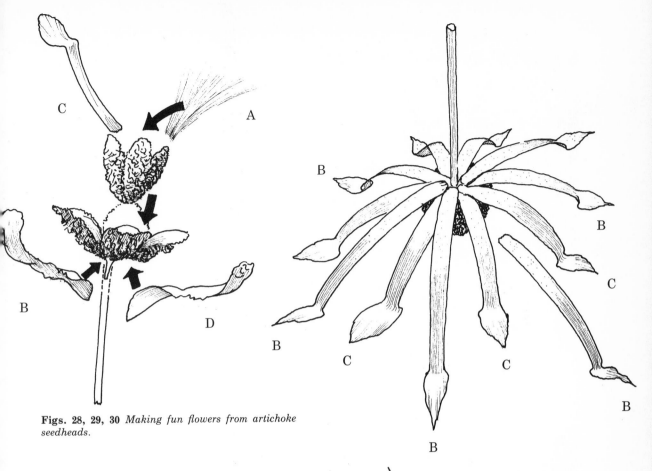

Figs. 28, 29, 30 *Making fun flowers from artichoke seedheads.*

For the flower in plate 59, choose a pine cone with the scales fully open. Cut out the centre and attach a wire for the flower stem. Position artichoke bracts from an inner row (c) between the scales of the pine cone to form two separate rows. Figure 30 shows how the bracts in one row are placed between those of the other row. Remember to keep the smooth inner surface facing the centre of the flower. To create a well balanced flower, it may be necessary to cut the bracts to shorten them slightly before sticking them in place. Stick four acanthus bracts round the cut-out centre of the cone. Finally, in the middle stick a carefully chosen Cape Gooseberry pod of an appropriate size (see page 98). This pod can of course be replaced by any other plant material that you happen to have, provided that it makes an effective-looking centre which is of the correct proportions to enable you to produce a well balanced flower.

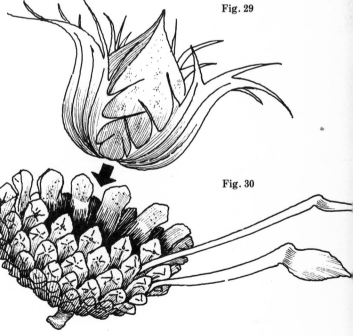

Fig. 29

Fig. 30

97

Lantern 'flowers'

Chinese Lantern and Cape Gooseberry are two of the common names for the plant *Physalis franchetii*. Its 'lanterns' are the inflated calyces which follow the flowers. The sprays of orange lanterns always remind me of the large arrangements seen in my childhood, when sprays of lanterns were arranged with beech leaves and fluffy pampas grasses.

Chinese Lanterns are easily dried by the air method (see page 157). I then cut the lanterns from the main stems, leaving a length of stalk on each one so that it can be wired as an individual lantern. Prepared in this way they are far more useful to the arranger than when they are left in rather ungainly sprawling sprays. What is more, a single spray will provide enough lanterns for an arrangement. To turn some of these lanterns into fun flowers can give added interest to an arrangement and provide yet another variation of form (fig. 31).

If you look at an individual lantern you will see that it has five ribbed divisions. With a small pair of sharp-pointed scissors, snip off the tip, and then insert the scissor point and cut down each rib in turn to form petals. To turn back the petals, gently massage each one between your thumb and forefinger.

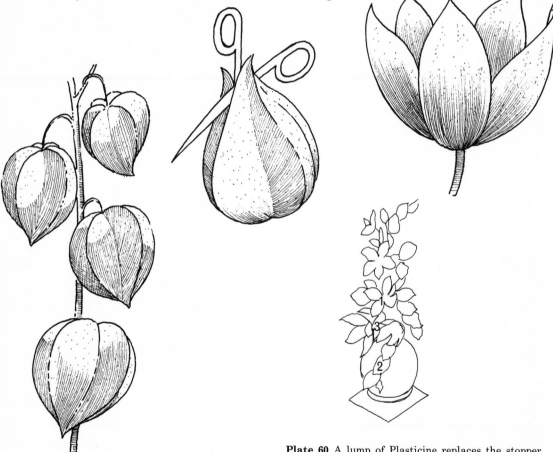

Fig. 31 *The inflated calyx of a Chinese Lantern is cut open to form an interesting flower-like shape.*

Plate 60 A lump of Plasticine replaces the stopper in this terracotta container, to hold an arrangement of lantern flowers with sprays and individual leaves of golden eleagnus, and the almost black leaves of *Garrya elliptica*.

Plate 61 A flower made from the inner seed discs of honesty. The centre is a cluster of phlomis calyces.

Plate 62 Another flower from inner seed discs of honesty, with a centre of hydrangea sepals.

Plate 63 A flower made from the outer seed discs. The purple colouring of the love-in-a-mist seedhead echoes the colouring of the honesty discs.

Plates 61, 62 and 63 The fun flowers shown here were made from honesty seedheads gathered during the summer, as soon as they were fully developed. At this stage the outer discs are flushed with delicate shades of mauve, while the inner discs are a delicate translucent green.

Honesty seed 'flowers'

Vases with bunches of honesty are reminiscent of the Victorian era. Although the inner discs of honesty seedheads have a beautiful translucent quality, stems of discs used in their entirety do little to inspire the flower arranger of today. But both the inner and outer discs can be used to make beautiful fun flowers. This is not my original idea, but I feel my approach may help to encourage the use of this common yet beautiful and unusual plant material.

To make the flowers illustrated in plates 61, 62 and 64, peel off the outer discs to reveal the inner translucent disc (fig. 32a). Stick the inner discs round the back of a central seedhead in as many rows as you want, to make single or double flowers (fig. 32b). For flowers of the type illustrated in plate 63, stick the outer discs round your chosen centre.

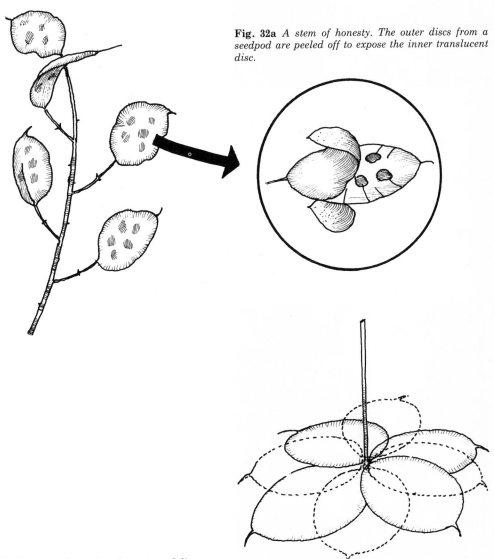

Fig. 32a *A stem of honesty. The outer discs from a seedpod are peeled off to expose the inner translucent disc.*

Fig. 32b *Making a fun flower from honesty seed discs.*

Plate 64 For the flowers in this arrangement I used
translucent inner discs taken from an honesty plant in
the autumn, when the outer discs are dry and papery.
The flowers are arranged in a candlecup holder which
is fitted into the neck of an alabaster container. The
texture of the alabaster is in perfect harmony with the
delicate flowers. For foliage I chose leaves of Solomon's
Seal, individually wired, which complement the flowers
in shape, colour and texture.

New flowers from old

The fun flowers shown in fig. 33 are suggestions for how you might use helichrysums which have reached the stage at which the centre discs of the florets have turned fluffy, a situation which I am quite sure must at some time arise with all growers of helichrysums—certainly with me it does. I think the flowers then look rather shabby and tatty. At this stage the seeds of the helichrysum have formed and are either ripe or ripening, and you will find it quite easy to pull out the fluffy middle with its attached seeds, leaving a nice smooth centre in which you can glue almost anything which is suitable in size and colour. (Incidentally, if you save the seeds they will provide next year's supply of helichrysums.) For centres I have used a seedhead of the oriental poppy, and a whorl of calyces cut from a stem of ballota.

Fig. 33 *Over-mature helichrysum flowers are transformed into fun flowers.*

Plate 65 The black-painted skeleton of an umbelliferous plant, with green autumn-gathered hydrangea sepals.

Plate 66 A white-sprayed umbelliferous skeleton, with pink summer-gathered hydrangea sepals.

Plate 67 An umbelliferous skeleton left its natural colour, with dark red autumn-gathered hydrangea sepals.

Plate 68 A gold-sprayed umbelliferous skeleton with blue summer-gathered hydrangea sepals.

From spring until autumn, the roadside banks provide the arranger of preserved flowers with many beautiful, interesting and useful, although often despised, plant materials. The common umbelliferous plants—cow parsley, ground elder and the rest—are particularly beautiful, and great favourites of mine. As winter approaches nature appears to have little left to offer as the banks become bare and uninteresting, and yet it was from this apparent bareness that inspiration for the flowers illustrated in plates 65, 66, 67 and 68 came to me. In a November hedgerow the umbelliferous plants that had provided a wealth of lace-like flowers for my delight throughout the summer stood tall and erect, bare skeletons, even the seeds swept away by the autumn winds. Many of the larger forms had become really tough and woody, and although at a glance they appeared just dead and dull, a closer look revealed not only the interesting branched formation of each head, but radiating from each the clusters of tiny stalks which bore the florets and in turn the seeds. I immediately saw these as clusters of stamens just crying out for petals. To emphasize this stamen-like effect, I painted some quite thickly, using a brush, allowing tiny droplets to form and give the appearance of pollen. For the others I wanted to achieve a more delicate effect and so I used a spray to paint them. Then I glued on petaloid hydrangea sepals for the petals (fig. 34).

Fig. 34 *Petaloid hydrangea sepals are glued to the skeleton branched stem of an umbelliferous seedhead.*

Leaf 'flowers'

I had carefully stored flowering spikes of horsetail for almost a year and still I had not decided how I could use them in an arrangement to their best advantage. Although I had put them into various woody scenes, their subdued colour plus the fact that the florets on each spike are so minute meant that they were overpowered by the other plant materials. While looking at my collection of plant materials with a view to more experimenting with fun flowers, I saw them in a completely new light. It happened that they were standing in a jar near a spike of glycerine-preserved Solomon's Seal. After preserving, the leaves of Solomon's Seal tend to go limp at the joint where each leaf joins the main stem, even if they are fully mature. For this reason I usually remove all the leaves and wire them individually (see page 18). The shape of the Solomon's Seal leaves with the flower spikes of the horsetail immediately made me think of the wild arum (which, incidentally, I have failed to preserve satisfactorily); I wrapped a leaf round a spike of horsetail (fig. 35b) and so another new flower was born! For the flowers in the arrangement I used the leaves from two separate spikes of Solomon's Seal; the paler ones are several years old and with age have turned this lovely limey green.

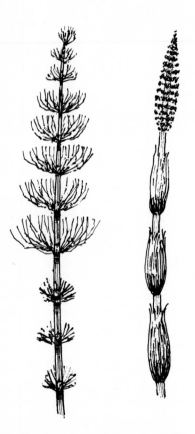

Fig. 35a *Non-flowering and flowering spikes of the wild horsetail plant.*

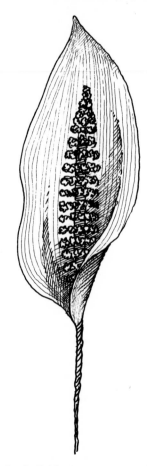

Fig. 35b *An individual leaf of Solomon's Seal is wrapped round a horsetail flower spike and wired to make a fun flower.*

Plate 69 Inspiration for arranging these lily-like fun flowers came from observing the natural habitat of wild arums; their solitary flower spikes enveloped in large spathes appear after the foliage has withered. Wild arums are usually found on damp shady banks or in woodlands. My lump of entwined tree root (a carefully hoarded find from a country walk) provided an ideal setting. As I found it difficult to use additional flowers or foliage without destroying the impact of the fun flowers and the beautiful form of the wood, I simply incorporated into the arrangement the trimmed, spiky, non-flowering stems of horsetail (fig. 35a) and some hypericum berries (see plate 28).

There are various reasons why I like using the leaves of the mountain ash to make fun flowers. The structure of the leaf is ideal— each leaf will provide sufficient petal-like segments to make a complete flower. The variation in size of the leaves means that you can make a natural-looking flower with irregular petals or, alternatively, the large and small segments from several leaves can be divided into groups to make large and small flowers. The range of colours of the autumn-gathered leaves, in addition to the green leaves of summer, makes it possible to have fun flowers that blend into different colour schemes.

To make flowers from mountain ash leaves, just stick the leaf segments round the back of your chosen centre (fig. 36). The fluffy centres of doronicum flowers, complete with stems, make particularly good centres for mountain ash flowers (see plate 9). They should be picked just as the petals have faded—if they are gathered late the centre will disintegrate. Rudbeckia centres make impressive-looking flowers (plate 70). These too should be picked as soon as the petals fade, or they will disintegrate.

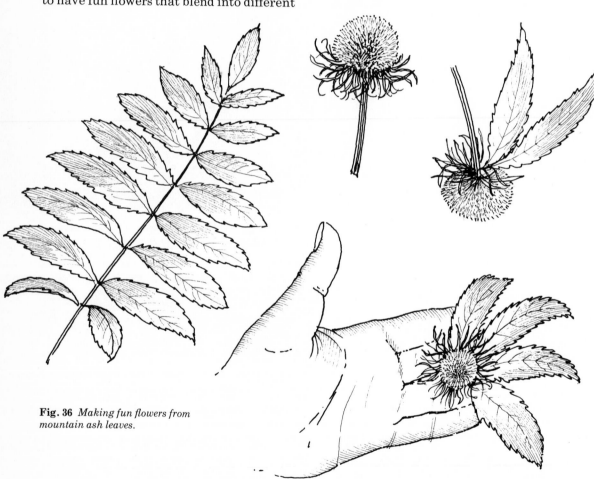

Fig. 36 *Making fun flowers from mountain ash leaves.*

Plate 70 For the centres of these flowers made from mountain ash leaves I chose the seedheads of rudbeckia flowers, complete with their stalks. To create a striking effect with the dark jug I used the almost black preserved foliage of *Garrya elliptica*.

Small leaves from almost any shrub are suitable for making daisy-like flowers. I made the sprays of flowers used in plate 54 from glycerined box leaves. In contrast, for the flowers in plate 71 I used the dark, almost black, glycerined leaves of escallonia. Through experimenting with a variety of combinations I discovered that the secret of success is to concentrate on using centres of a contrasting colour. I used alder cones as centres for the box leaf flowers, and the escallonia leaf flowers have golden santolina (lavender cotton) flowers as centres.

The two flowers described are very easy to make. The box leaf flowers are made by sticking the leaves between the tiny scales of alder cones, about a third of the way up from the stem. It is necessary to lengthen the stem of the alder cones as described on page 62. For the escallonia leaf flowers, the leaves are simply stuck round the back of the centres.

Plate 71 One of my favourite figurines, encircled by an arrangement of fun flowers made from escallonia leaves with santolina centres (1), arranged with glycerined box (2) and choisya (3) leaves. This subtle and unusual combination of colours would make an interesting feature in any room and would harmonize with any furnishings.

110

6 Special effects for special occasions

Traditionally, flowers play an important part in the celebration of many special occasions. I do not for one moment suggest that preserved flowers should entirely replace fresh flowers on such occasions, but one or two preserved arrangements can be a very worthwhile addition to the decorations. Preserved flowers have the advantage that they can be collected and preserved over a period of several months, when flowers of the appropriate colourings —or flowers which are especially appropriate for some other reason—are plentiful in the garden. Even if you are without access to garden flowers it is still a good idea to preserve some flowers in advance, for in-season flowers at florists' or in the markets are always much cheaper. And, of course, you avoid the awful frustration of not being able to buy the right flowers at the right time. With this in mind, I have devoted this chapter to my own ideas for just a few of these special occasions: a wedding, a golden wedding anniversary, a ruby wedding, a birthday, and Christmas. I hope my designs will spark off other ideas in your own mind as to how preserved flowers could be used in association with your own very special occasion.

Flowers preserved before or after the event also have the great advantage that they can provide that something extra special to be kept and cherished long after, when memories and photographs are otherwise all that remain of the great day. A picture made up of preserved flowers and protected by glass will provide an even longer-lasting memento than an arrangement, and will continue to give pleasure for many years—it may even be handed down as a family heirloom, and become one of tomorrow's antiques!

A wedding

To use only preserved arrangements for a wedding would be neither desirable nor practical, but the idea of one carefully positioned preserved arrangement has great potential, particularly for a winter wedding. Not all brides can be June brides, but it is possible for the bride's favourite flowers from a June garden to accompany her on her wedding day. Again, special associations could spark off ideas for preserving and using particular flowers; for example, you could preserve flowers that have a link with the bride's name, or maybe flowers connected with a relative or friend.

An arrangement of preserved garden flowers is often a particularly appropriate choice for the decoration on top of the wedding cake (plate 73). There are far more garden flowers of an appropriate size than there are among typical florists' flowers.

A tiny spray of preserved flowers can be assembled and stuck in one corner of each place card—and I am sure guests would delight in keeping their cards as lasting souvenirs.

Although the colour schemes in plates 72 and 73 are based on those of a traditional white wedding, the ideas could of course be copied in any chosen colour. It has to be admitted, however, that of all preserved flowers white and cream are my favourites. There always seem to be many more white flowers that preserve well than flowers of any other colour. When preserved the different types of flowers develop quite distinct shades of white through to cream.

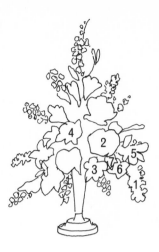

Plate 73 The dainty arching sprays of *Spiraea arguta* (1) form the outline of this arrangement for the top of a wedding cake. The other flowers used are roses (2), philadelphus (3), freesias (4) and miniature orchids (5), with, recessed between them, green hydrangea florets (6) and tiny variegated ivy leaves (7). A traditional silver cake vase holds the arrangement.

Plate 72 I chose this candlestick for my arrangement for two reasons. First, its shape suggested an elegant style of arrangement and, secondly, its colouring harmonized with my selection of cream flowers. The single variety of lilac called 'Primrose' (1) and sprays of *Spiraea arguta* (Bridal Wreath) (2), form the outline of my arrangement; the other flowers used are dahlias (3), feverfew daisies (4), spray carnations (5) and the beautiful cream flowers of the single hollyhock (6). Green hosta (7) and montbretia leaves (8) echo the colouring of the hollyhock centres.

113

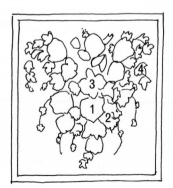

Plate 74 Flowers from a bridal bouquet preserved and mounted as a picture. The bouquet was taken to pieces and the wire stems were discarded, together with any damaged flowers. After preserving, the flowers were arranged on a background of cream silk in a design which closely resembled the bouquet. The flowers include roses (1), spray carnations (2) and alstroemeria (3); the only foliage in the bouquet is variegated ivy leaves (4).

A recessed shape for a picture frame

Readers of my previous books will already know that for many years I have had the pleasure of preserving the flowers from brides' and bridesmaids' bouquets. After preserving them I re-create the shape of the bouquet in the form of a picture in a recessed picture frame which is then protected by glass (plate 74). It is quite easy to increase the depth of a standard picture or photograph frame so that it will accommodate preserved flowers: just make a recessed shape to fit behind the frame.

You will need the following materials:

Stiff cardboard
Fabric for lining the shape
PVA or latex glue, or an aerosol glue
Contact adhesive
Glass for the frame
Thin, pliable card
Screw eyes for hanging

First, measure the inside of the rebate on the back of your frame (fig. 37a), and determine what depth of frame you need to accommodate your flowers. Cut four strips of stiff cardboard of a length to fit inside the rebate and wide enough to deepen the frame by the amount necessary. To allow for the thickness of the cardboard, cut the strips for the top and bottom of the frame (B) slightly shorter than the rebate measurement. To make the frame less box-like, mitre the ends of the strips of card as shown in fig. 37b. Glue the pieces of card together, positioning the top and bottom pieces (B) inside the side pieces (A), as in fig. 37c.

Cut a piece of cardboard (or hardboard) to fit the back of the recessed shape. Glue it in position inside your strips of card (fig. 37d).

Cut out a fabric lining for your recessed shape. Make sure that the fabric is cut on the straight of the weave, or you will have difficulty in getting it to lie smoothly. Using sharp scissors, cut a v in each corner (fig. 37e). Glue the fabric inside the recessed shape, pushing the edges of the corners together to make a neat join. A PVA or latex glue is suitable for sticking almost all fabrics. For the very thinnest fabrics, however, it is best to use an aerosol glue.

Position your flowers on the fabric. When you are satisfied with the arrangement, stick them in place, using a quick-drying contact adhesive (fig. 37f). Apply the glue to the flowers, not to the background.

If the original frame does not have any glass, get your glass merchant to cut a piece to size. Make sure the glass is quite clean before you place it in the rebate. Position the recessed shape behind the frame. Cut four strips of thin, pliable card and glue them over the join between the frame and the recessed shape, to seal them together (fig. 37g). Insert screw eyes for hanging.

A golden wedding

A golden wedding in the family is an occasion that is always discussed well in advance. Let us suppose the event will take place during the winter months, when there is very little choice of golden flowers available in the garden. It would be easy enough to pop along to the florist for chrysanthemums or roses, which are always expensive in winter, but it is much more fun to plan ahead during the summer and autumn to preserve and store such flowers as rudbeckias, roses, freesias, dahlias and statice. A little preliminary investigation may reveal the couple's favourite flowers.

An idea which can give great pleasure is to find a way of gathering some flowers from the couple's own garden and to preserve and store them until their special day, when you will be able to surprise them with a lasting arrangement.

You may happen to have a suitable container, or perhaps you may like to buy one as part of the gift, but personally I always welcome the excuse to design and make a container for such an occasion. I used the decorative forms of scallop shells as the basis for the container of the table arrangement shown in plate 75. Not only is there practically no cost involved, but an individually designed container such as this I am sure will be received with greater affection by the couple.

(a)

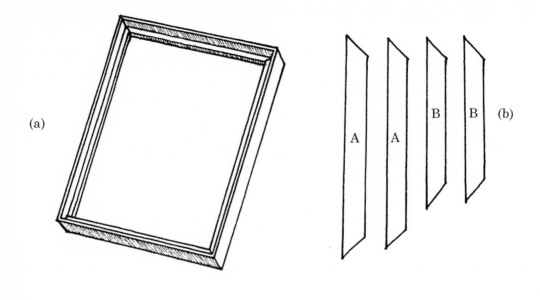

(b)

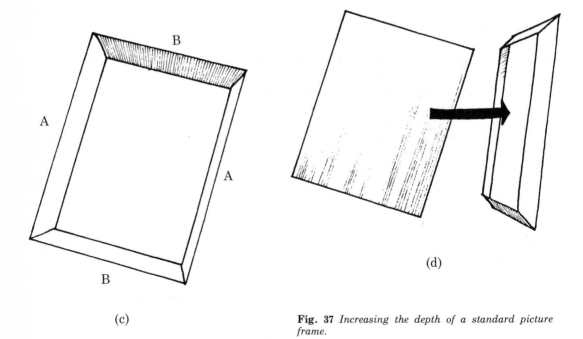

(c)

(d)

Fig. 37 *Increasing the depth of a standard picture frame.*

(e)

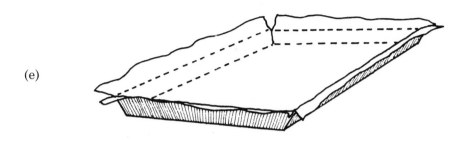

(f)

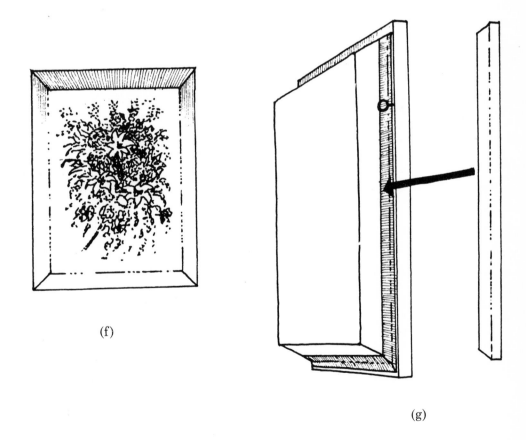

(g)

A container based on scallop shells

Only a few simple materials are needed for the scallop shell container:

> Some strong, stiff cardboard
> PVA or latex glue
> A small round plastic box, such as an empty margarine carton
> A strip of velvet about 125 mm (5 in) wide
> 4 scallop shells
> About 1.4 m (1½ yards) of gold cord— embroidery cord is ideal, but parcel cord would do

Cut three strips of cardboard about 20 mm (¾ in) wide, two of equal length and one just under twice as long. Glue the longest strip (A) across the open side of the plastic box, then glue the other two strips (B and C) at right angles to A, to form a cross shape (fig. 38a). When this construction is dry it can be painted brown, or any other dark colour, depending on the chosen colour scheme.

Cut a round cardboard shape about 12 mm (½ in) wider than the carton. Cover this shape with velvet in the way described for base number 3 on page 45, then stick the covered shape on the bottom of the container. Cover the inside of each shell with a smear of glue and mould and press a piece of velvet into position. Trim away surplus velvet close to the edge of each shell and glue gold cord round the edge (fig. 38b). Position the shells on the cardboard cross strips, as shown in fig. 38c, and glue them firmly in place.

Your arrangement should be made in a small container which is roughly the size of the box used for the base—I used another margarine carton. Position it on top of the velvet-covered shape.

Plate 75 Golden roses (1), freesias (2), statice (3), rudbeckias (4) and golden rod flowers (5) were arranged with leaves from the golden form of cypress (6) and the dark brown leaves of forsythia (7) in a shallow plastic container. The candle was pushed into the block of flower foam to anchor it firmly before the flowers were arranged. The finished arrangement was carefully positioned on the shell container.

Fig. 38 *Making a scallop shell container for an arrangement.*

(a)

(b)

(c)

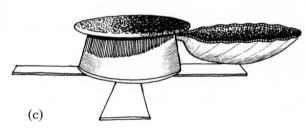

Plate 76 Red roses arranged with their own leaves on a white velvet background make up this ruby wedding picture.

Plate 77 On this heart-shaped plaque red and white helichrysums are arranged with perennial statice on a background of echinops leaves. The lovely silvery undersides of the leaves are far more attractive than their top sides, so they are arranged with the undersides uppermost.

A ruby wedding

Red roses are the obvious flowers to choose for a ruby wedding. You might like to try preserving the roses and making them into a picture as a lasting keepsake. It is advisable to place the picture in a recessed frame with a glazed front, to protect the flowers. Instructions for converting a standard photograph frame into a frame with a suitable recess can be found on page 115.

Everlasting flowers, such as helichrysums and statice, and flowers with small florets, are sufficiently resilient to be used for a plaque, without any protective glass. When contemplating a gift of preserved flowers for a ruby wedding, I immediately felt that I would like to present them on rich red velvet. This decided, it seemed obvious for such an occasion to create a heart-shaped plaque. I had made heart-shaped plaques before, but this time I wanted to incorporate as a feature the light and dark effect that the surface of velvet produces when it is held at different angles. Ruching seemed the best way to achieve this. Plate 77 illustrates the result, a padded heart shape enclosed within a ruched heart-shaped surround. Step-by-step details for making up and assembling the plaque are given overleaf.

A heart-shaped plaque

You will need the following materials:

Rigid cardboard
Padding, such as wadding or plastic foam
PVA or latex glue
Red velvet—the exact amount will of course depend on the size of plaque you want to make, but for a plaque 190 mm ($7\frac{1}{2}$ in) deep and the same across at the widest point, I used 230 mm ($\frac{1}{4}$ yard) of velvet
Paper or thin card
Contact adhesive
A ring for hanging

Cut a heart shape from the cardboard. Cut a piece of padding to the same shape as the cardboard but smaller, to allow for the ruched surround. Glue the padding in place on the cardboard (fig. 39a).

Cut a piece of velvet large enough to allow for turnings. Lay the unpadded side of the cardboard down on the velvet, and trim the velvet to within 12 mm ($\frac{1}{2}$ in) of the cardboard all round. Cut notches all round. Turn the notched edge over and glue it down on the back of the cardboard shape (fig. 39b).

Cut a cardboard outline shape for the ruched surround. This should be the shape and size of the cardboard heart and the width of the distance between the edge of the heart and the padding (fig. 39c).

Cut a strip of velvet twice the width of the cardboard surround (fig. 39d), run a gathering thread along each edge and pull it up as tight as possible (fig. 39e). It may be necessary to join several strips together. Position the ruched velvet round the cardboard shape and oversew it to the velvet on the reverse side (fig. 39f). Close stitching is necessary, but the neatness or otherwise of the stitching is not too important, as it will be hidden. To neaten the back of the finished heart, stick on a piece of paper or thin card cut to shape.

Arrange your plant materials on the velvet and stick them in place with contact adhesive.

Attach a hanging ring (obtainable from art and crafts shops) to the back.

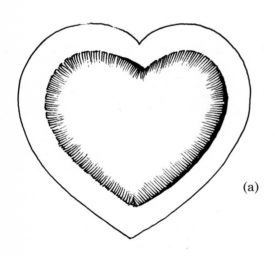

(a)

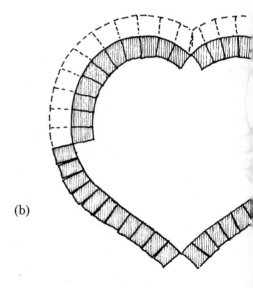

(b)

Fig. 39 *Making a heart-shaped plaque.*

(c)

(d)

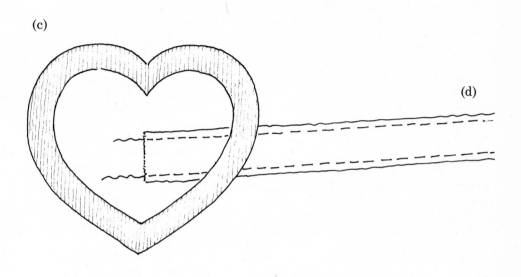

(e)

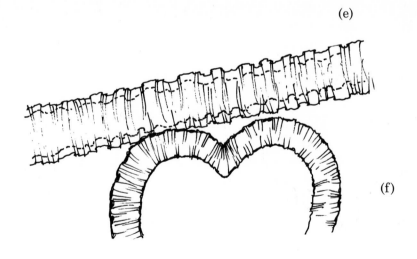

(f)

123

Plate 78 The beautiful creamy-white heads of wild elder, which resemble a tracery of lace, inspired me to create this picture. I used both the buds (1) and the fully opened florets (2) in the border design. The white flowers and florets which form the central and corner arrangements include cornflowers (3), zinnias (4), deutzia flowers (5), saxifrages (6), Japanese Anemones (7), statice (8), *Spiraea arguta* (9) and feverfew daisies (10).

124

A birthday

The picture shown in plate 78 was made as a gift for a hundredth birthday—a very special occasion indeed! Many flower arrangers are also keen embroiderers, which is not surprising as many aspects of flower arranging have much in common with embroidery. A picture such as the one illustrated, which is more of a design than an arrangement, closely resembles a piece of embroidery. Instead of creating flower shapes with stitchery, I used real flowers that I had preserved. Pictures both large and small can be designed and made up using a variety of small flowers and florets. If you do not feel able to work out your own design, why not either copy or adapt an embroidery design? When you are satisfied with the positioning of your flowers, apply a dab of contact adhesive to each one and stick it in place. For long-lasting protection from dust and itchy fingers, a picture like this will need to be set in a recessed glazed frame (see page 115).

Painting plant materials

I hesitate to advise painting plant materials, and I do so with certain reservations. In general I much prefer natural colouring in preserved flowers and other plant materials, but I have come to see that painted material has its own attractions. I would, however, restrict its use to certain special circumstances.

Painting is a useful way to create an effect. There are two obvious occasions for doing just that; one is in competitive work, particularly in an abstract class—but often such work is not suitable for use in the home. The other reason is for the celebration of a special day, such as Christmas. I would like to emphasize the word 'effect', to stress that before reaching for a can of spray paint and spraying everything gold or silver, or any other colour that may take your fancy, you should give careful consideration to what you are about to spray and what effect you would like to achieve. For example, I wanted the cone in plate 85 to resemble a porcelain ornament and so I sprayed the completed arrangement with several coats of paint. In contrast, in the arrangement illustrated in plate 81 I painted individual flowers. Sometimes it can be more effective to paint only parts of each piece of plant material—this is what I did with the fun flowers in plate 80, for example. There are no rules about what to paint or how much painted plant material to use in an arrangement, and I do not intend to try and make any. I just hope that my own ideas may interest readers and encourage them to experiment with this medium.

It is a good idea to keep a box to which faded and rejected plant materials which are past their best for natural preserved work can be banished. This will provide a source of materials for painting.

It is up to the individual arranger whether he prefers to apply paint with a spray or a brush, but as a general guide it is easier to spray such materials as fir cones and helichrysums—covering each tiny scale or bract, and especially in between them, is such a tedious job with a brush. Again, many seedheads are of such a delicate structure that trying to apply paint with a brush would certainly damage them.

Plate 79 This close-up of one of the fun flowers in plate 80 shows how gold paint can effectively be applied to parts of a rather colourless fun flower to create a more striking effect. (See page 95 for details of how these flowers are made.)

Plate 80 This unusual colour scheme was created using only three desiccant-preserved flowers. The roses were arranged with gilded fun flowers made from artichoke bracts, and naturally dried mahonia berries; although these berries become rather shrivelled when dried, this is more than compensated for by the grape-like bloom and colouring they retain. The golden cypress, which turns slightly brown when dried naturally, echoes the colouring of the container. The brass-like effect of the container was achieved by the method described on page 36. Raw umber oil paint was used as a base, with gold paste rubbed on to create the highlighting and show up the embossed pattern of the container.

126

A Christmas table arrangement

A combination of painted and natural preserved plant materials makes a charming arrangement for a Christmas table.

The stand for the arrangement shown in plate 81 is similar to the miniature two-tier stand in plate 49. It is easy to make, and could of course also be used at other times of the year for a preserved arrangement in natural colours.

To make the stand you will need the following materials:

> A small amount of cellulose filler (such as Polyfilla) or modelling plaster (the self-hardening type)
> A 200 mm (8 in) disc of wood or very thick, rigid cardboard
> The top of a washing-up liquid bottle
> A 250 mm (10 in) length of dowelling

Fabric or crêpe paper to cover the base (I used green crêpe paper to match the Christmas crackers)
> A cake doily
> Contact adhesive
> Thin card
> Half a large ball of flower foam
> Half a small ball of flower foam

Mix the filler or plaster with a little water to the consistency of a stiff dough. Mould it into a rough mound and position it in the centre of the wooden or cardboard disc. Push the bottle top firmly over it, making sure there is enough plaster to fill the top and hold it firmly in place. Push the dowelling through the neck of the bottle top and into the plaster (fig. 40a). Leave the stand overnight to set firmly, then paint the stick in a colour to tone with your arrangement.

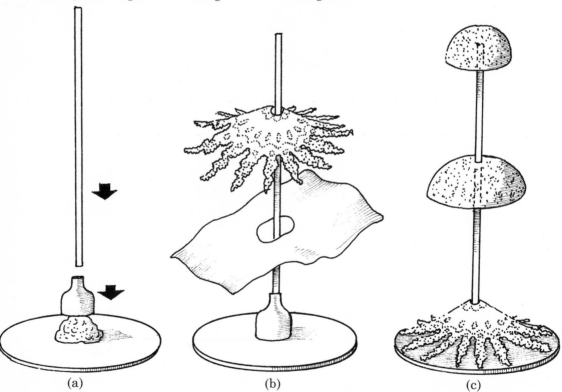

(a)   (b)   (c)

Fig. 40 *Making a two-tier container for a table arrangement.*

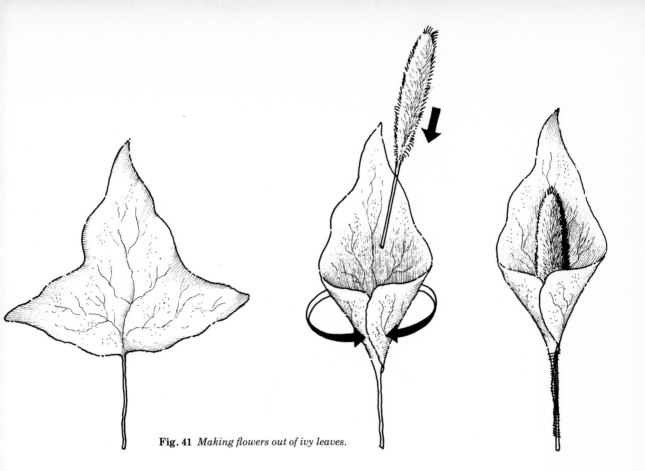

Fig. 41 *Making flowers out of ivy leaves.*

Cut a piece of fabric or crêpe paper slightly larger than the base to allow for turning over. Make notches round the edge. Cut a hole in the centre and slide the cover down the dowelling. Cut a hole in the centre of the doily and slide this down over the covered base (fig. 40b). (To create a link with my painted ferns, I cut away part of the doily, leaving only a fern-like shape radiating from the centre.) Turn over the notched edge of the cover and glue it down. Stick thin card over the back of the disc, for a neat finish.

Push the dowelling up through the large half-ball of flower foam. Glue the ball in position half-way up the stick. Finish off the stand by pushing the top of the stick part-way into the small half-ball of foam (fig. 40c).

To make the flowers shown in the arrangement in plate 81 overleaf you will need ivy leaves, grasses, gold and white paint and some glitter powder. I used fresh ivy leaves, because they could easily be bent into the flower shape. Desiccant-preserved leaves are too brittle to bend, and if glycerined leaves were used it might be difficult to get the paint to adhere to the leaf surface. Although the flowers do not last as long as they would if they were made with desiccant- or glycerine-preserved leaves, I find the paint covering keeps them in good condition well beyond the Christmas season.

Spray grasses with gold paint. Sprinkle them with glitter while the paint is still wet, then allow them to dry.

Fold in the two sides of the lower part of each leaf. Overlap them slightly and stick them to each other as shown in fig. 41. When the adhesive is dry, paint the leaves with white paint, using a spray or a brush. Allow at least twenty-four hours for the paint to dry, then push a glittered grass down the central vein of each leaf. Wire the leaf and the grass stalk together and bind them (page 23).

Decorating crackers

Plain, inexpensive crackers can be transformed into decorative accessories to use with a Christmas table arrangement. Not only will they provide a talking point for your Christmas party, but you can be sure your guests will want to cut off the decorations to take them home to treasure long after the festive season is over.

For each cracker, cut an oblong of thin card to form a base for your plant materials. When you have arranged the materials to your satisfaction, glue them on the card. If you use a quick-drying contact adhesive, you will be able to fix some of the plant materials in an upright position. It may be necessary to use smaller materials than the ones used in the table arrangement. For instance, I used slightly smaller ivy leaves for my flowers, and smaller helichrysums. You can either glue the decorated card in position on top of the existing cracker motif, or remove the motif and glue the decoration in its place. To provide continuity between table arrangement and crackers I used small pieces cut from a matching cake doily to trim the ends of each cracker. I simply glued these on and then cut the cracker edge to correspond with the decorative shape made by the doily shapes.

Plates 81 and 82 The materials for both the table arrangement and the cracker decorations are scarlet helichrysums 'Hot Bikini', gold-painted ferns and quaking grasses, and white-painted lily-like fun flowers with small sprigs of cypress foliage recessed between them. In the table arrangement the formation of the fern fronds is repeated in the gold cake doily. A scarlet tablecloth would both tone with the red helichrysums and create a rich and vibrant effect for a festive party.

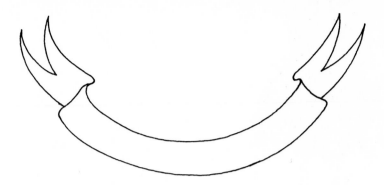

Fig. 42 *The paper ribbon for the Christmas plaque illustrated in plate 83.*

A Christmas greetings plaque

You will find a Christmas greetings message in the form of a plaque decorated with preserved flowers will be around long after the other Christmas cards have been committed to the wastepaper basket or become scraps in a scrapbook. My idea for the plaque illustrated in plate 83 was based on the rather elaborate greetings cards of the Victorian era. I think it is fun to base an idea on past treasures, and from my interpretation I hope you will be inspired to create your own.

The plaque itself was made in exactly the same way as the plaque described on page 66. A gold twisted embroidery cord was carefully glued round the edge of the completed base.

The paper ribbon shape in fig. 42 is given actual size, to enable readers who wish to make a plaque of the same size to trace and reproduce it.

Plate 83 A Christmas greetings plaque. A selection of tiny grasses, ferns and seedheads were all sprayed with gold paint before being arranged with natural tiny white everlasting flowers of the perennial plant anaphalis, on a base covered with red velvet. The plaque measures 200 × 150 mm (8 × 6 in).

A special present

An arrangement is always a welcome gift, and a preserved arrangement has the great advantage that it is long-lasting. I have chosen to illustrate, as a gift appropriate for almost any occasion, an arrangement of preserved seedheads, leaves and cones from a variety of trees. These can of course be left their natural colours (plate 84). Alternatively, the completed cone can be painted to resemble porcelain and used as a permanent ornament (plate 85). China ornaments in the form of fruits, flowers or other plant materials displayed in a dish or on a stand can be very attractive but very expensive to buy. To make your own is a little time-consuming, but involves little cost and is certainly more exciting.

Even if the finished cone is not painted, the very fact that the plant materials are so close together means that plant materials of different shapes and forms must be used. As the arrangement is intended as a long-lasting ornament, it is important to choose materials which have a firm structure; for example, most deciduous foliage would be too flimsy, so use evergreen foliage. Delicate seedheads should be avoided and only those which dry to an almost woody texture used.

133

Plate 84 A variety of cones provided the basic ingredients for my arrangement; these include cedar (1), cypress (2), pine (3) and larch (4) cones. Seedpods of poppies (5), peonies (6) and cardoon thistles (7), together with a few beech nuts (8) give additional interest of shape and form. The seedheads of tansy (9) and leaves of the evergreen *Garrya elliptica* (10) provide a complete contrast, which is necessary to prevent the arrangement from appearing too solid.

Making up the cone

A basic flower foam cone shape (fig. 43) is generally available from florists, particularly at Christmas time. If you have any difficulty finding one you can cut your own shape out of flower foam. I anchored my cone in an inexpensive plastic container with prongs, designed to hold either this or

Fig. 43 *A flower foam cone is anchored on the prongs of an inexpensive plastic container.*

the rounded foam shape shown in fig. 3. Alternatively, you can use any china dish or stand in which a prong shape (fig. 3f) can be fixed to hold the foam. Some plant materials can be used as they are, but others will need wiring. Evergreen leaves have to be removed from their branches and wired individually (see page 18). And cones, which seldom have any more than a stump of stem, will usually need to be wired (see page 61). In an arrangement such as this it is important that each piece of plant material remains firmly in place, so for extra security apply a dab of glue to the end of each stem or wire before pushing it into the foam. Graduate the size of your plant materials, using smaller sizes at the top and increasing the size as you move downwards.

To paint the cone I used an aerosol can of car paint in one of the many off-white or cream shades. I prefer these to brilliant white. It will be necessary to spray the cone at least three times, maybe more. Do not apply too much paint at any one time.

Plate 85 Here the arrangement illustrated in plate 84 has been sprayed with several coats of car paint, to achieve a porcelain effect.

Reference section

Index of plant materials

Part of plant

b	berries	f	flowers
br	bracts	g	grasses
c	cones	l	leaves
cl	calyces	n	nuts
ct	catkins	s	seedheads

Method of preserving

A Air   D Desiccant   G Glycerine

Numbers refer to the plates in which the plant materials are illustrated. For ease of reference in this plant list individual varieties of plants have been grouped to-gether under the common family name.

All the plant materials shown in the illustrations are listed here in alphabetical order, with a reference to the methods I used to preserve each one.

However, in the captions to the plates you will find details of all plant varieties used in the arrangements.

138

The methods of preserving

For simplicity and ease of reference, the methods and details of preserving the plant materials used throughout the book are grouped together in this reference section. The step-by-step diagrams make it easy for the reader to follow through the various stages, from picking to storing. Even beginners should have no difficulty in producing successful results from the very first attempt, although they will of course improve with practice.

Preserving with desiccants

A desiccant is a substance which absorbs moisture. Sand, alum, cornmeal, starch, detergent powders, borax powder and silica gel are all desiccants. However, a desiccant used for plant preservation must not only absorb moisture but absorb it quickly, to enable the natural colouring of the plant material to be retained. A slow preserving process usually results in loss of colour.

The two products which I have used with the greatest success are silica gel and borax powder, but, as with all craft products, it is advisable to experiment for yourself, particularly as the conditions under which you preserve must also be taken into consideration. As a guide for readers who have no previous experience with desiccants, I will explain the advantages and disadvantages I have found silica gel and borax to have.

Silica gel

Silica gel, which absorbs up to 50 per cent of its own weight in moisture, is used industrially for moisture absorption. It looks rather like granulated sugar. Silica gel is more expensive than borax, but it has the advantage that, unlike borax, it does not demand heat during use.

It is often difficult to obtain a suitable grade of crystals, as the standard grade sold by chemists and drug stores is usually too large and heavy, and would cause delicate plant materials to become distorted. The intense hardness of these crystals makes them unsuitable for crushing, even in an electric grinder, so it is best to buy crystals sold specifically for the purpose of preserving plant material. These are sold under a variety of trade names and usually contain silica gel of a more refined grade than the standard crystals. On account of the difficulty I myself have experienced in locating and recommending retail sources for preserving crystals, I now market my own brand of crystals (see page 160 for details).

Silica gel and preserving crystals should always be stored in an airtight tin, to keep them dry.

From time to time crystals will become fully charged with their maximum amount of moisture. They will not actually feel wet, and different brands of crystals show their moisture content in different ways, so always check the instructions given with the crystals you are using. The most usual indication is a colour change. For example, the flower crystals I market lose their blue colouring and become a dirty pink. When this happens the crystals can be reactivated as follows.

Pour the crystals into a shallow pan and put them in a warm 120°C (250°F or gas mark $\frac{1}{2}$) oven. Stir them occasionally to ensure even drying. After fifteen to thirty minutes the blue colour will reappear, indicating that the crystals are dry. Turn off the oven and leave the crystals in the oven for a further half-hour or so to cool slightly. Then return them to their storage tin. Replace the lid of the tin immediately, before the crystals start to absorb any moisture from the air. Do not attempt to preserve flowers in the crystals until they are quite cold.

If they are reactivated in this way when necessary, silica gel crystals can be used over and over again. They will last for an indefinite period.

Borax

Household borax is a powder which is obtainable relatively inexpensively from chemists and drug stores. It does have certain disadvantages. During use a constant dry heat of approximately 24°C (75°F) must be maintained to obtain successful results. Borax also has a tendency to cling—the specks of powder are particularly noticeable on dark-coloured materials. The particles can be brushed off fairly easily, however. Again, many flowers, such as roses, will not preserve successfully in borax; because it does not draw out the moisture as efficiently and rapidly as silica gel, they tend to lose colour.

Borax can be stored anywhere dry. A cardboard box or a paper bag makes a perfectly adequate container. But when you use borax, do make sure it is completely dry. Unless it is quite dry and free from lumps, plant materials will not preserve successfully. The powder should run through your fingers like table salt. If it clings together and is inclined to be lumpy, spread it out on a shallow tray and leave it in a warm place, such as an airing cupboard, to dry.

Using desiccants to preserve flowers

If you want to create a flower arrangement that does not have that typically dried look, the two characteristics to aim for are colour impact and the retention of each flower's natural form. Both colour and shape are most effectively preserved by desiccants. Desiccants enable us to preserve flowers that cannot be successfully preserved by any other method. And it is

difficult to put into words the charm of, for example, three preserved water lilies casually arranged in a glass dish in January (see plate 19), or one peony arranged with its own foliage, to emphasize the intricate beauty and colour of a single flower which during its season in the garden is so often only appreciated in the mass (see plate 20). Just six yellow lilies were sufficient desiccant-preserved flowers to create the arrangement in plate 34. These examples also illustrate that for the beginner, and often for those with experience in flower arranging too, restraint is the keynote in the use of desiccant-preserved flowers. This is fortunate, as if you preserve too many flowers you will almost certainly find that you have storage problems. Remember, it is much better to have a smaller collection of preserved flowers that can be properly stored and cared for than large quantities that become squashed and damaged because the storage space is inadequate.

Choosing flowers suitable for desiccant preserving

I find that the beginner so often wants to preserve the flowers that are the least suitable for preserving. You will recall that evergreen leaves have a much firmer structure than deciduous ones. Well, flowers are much the same, some flower petals have a much stronger and firmer tissue structure than others. Daisy-type flowers are a good example. I would advise concentrating on these to begin with. When you feel confident in the technique, you can experiment with the more delicate blooms. With experience, one becomes able to judge the chances of success just by looking at and feeling the petals of a flower. The flowers illustrated throughout this book will serve as a guide to which flowers can be preserved successfully.

Colour changes in desiccant-preserved flowers

Some flowers develop slight colour changes during the preserving process and while some preserved flowers stand the test of time displayed in an arrangement, others mellow or literally fade. Personally, I think it is fun just to accept any colour change that may occur during the preserving of garden flowers.

A preserved flower arrangement can be as full of colour as an arrangement of fresh flowers, but if for every flower in a preserved arrangement an identical flower was picked for a fresh arrangement and then the two arrangements were compared, the overall colour effect would be different. The preservation process can intensify the strength of colour in some flowers while weakening it in others. If you start with, say, a red or a yellow flower, after preserving you will still have a red or a yellow flower, but the tone of the colour may have changed; so the tonal value of the preserved arrangement will differ from that of the fresh arrangement. For me this adds interest and excitement to preserving. And, after all, the tone of fresh flowers in the garden changes, both between the bud stage and the fully mature flower and according to the degree and strength of sunlight.

Stability of colour

It would be very convenient if I were able to list the colours that under perfect conditions remain stable for months or even years after preserving, but to attempt this could cause total frustration. For example, let us look at blue flowers. Delphiniums, cornflowers and forget-me-nots appear to retain their true colour indefinitely—I have some that are now fifteen years old and still good. I find, however, that a blue campanula will fade to white after only a month or so. Pink flowers in general lose their colour intensity after a few months, at which time they are lovely to use in soft, subdued colour schemes. Red appears to be unpredictable but in fact shades of red basically fall into two groups: orange or yellow-reds last well and should be used when a clear, bright red is required. Blue-reds, that is magenta, rose or pinky reds, tend to darken considerably as the blue undertone is accentuated. Most yellow flowers, I find, are very reliable. Many white flowers tend to turn cream, which is really very pleasing as cream is not so dominant when arranged with other colours.

Using desiccants to preserve leaves

The glycerine method is usually considered the obvious way to preserve foliage, but although this method produces beautifully pliable preserved leaves, its use is restricted to fully mature leaves. Immature leaves will not preserve successfully by the glycerine method, and nor will leaves which have begun to develop their autumn colours. And glycerine preserving always produces a fairly marked change in the colouring of the leaves. As we have discussed, this can be an advantage, as the different colours produced by preserving extend the range of colours available to the arranger. However, if you want to retain the natural colouring of the leaves you must use the desiccant method. There are four groups of leaves in which the retention of the natural colourings may be particularly desirable: leaves which have developed their autumn colours; immature spring leaves; silver leaves; leaves which have beautiful markings or veining.

I find that in general it is thin-textured deciduous leaves that are best suited to desiccant preserving. Evergreen leaves do not on the whole preserve well by this method. Variegated ivy leaves are an exception, but even with these it is a good idea to preserve more than you need: I rarely get 100 per cent success. With variegated ivy it is advisable to pick mature leaves, as the immature leaves are usually more fleshy. Remember, all desiccant-preserved leaves are fragile and therefore require careful handling. The special spray coating recommended for flowers on page 150 is ideal for use on smooth-surfaced, desiccant-preserved leaves, rendering them more pliable. It also gives them a sheen, a great advantage in our attempt to create preserved arrangements with a fresh look.

142

Desiccant preserving step by step

If you want perfect desiccant-preserved flowers, then I am afraid you must be prepared to sacrifice their all-too-short lives as fresh flowers, the reason being that it is most important to gather flowers before they begin to develop seedpods. When this stage is reached in the life cycle of a flower, although at a glance it may look perfect, the petals are in fact either beginning to fade or loosen in preparation for falling off. If the petals are at all loose, they will almost certainly fall off after preserving. Many large-petalled flowers, such as roses, in fact preserve far more successfully if they are picked before they are fully open. Figure 44a shows a rose just ready to be picked for preserving. Figure 44b shows the stage at which a bloom is likely to shatter when preserved. If, however, for some reason a flower needs to be preserved at the loose-petalled stage, with patience it is possible to glue the petals carefully back on (see page 149).

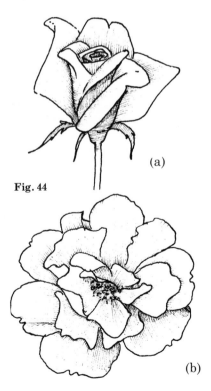

(a)

Fig. 44

(b)

The ideal flowers for preserving are those which are picked fresh from the garden. They should be gathered when they are dry, without any trace of dew or rain. Even flowers that appear dry on the surface often retain moisture deep down between their petals—this is frequently the case with roses. A good shake will reveal any hidden moisture. Flowers preserved wet will inevitably turn brown. Do not gather flowers at mid-day in full sun during hot weather, as the petals will be limp. This means the formation of the petals cannot be satisfactorily retained—petals must be firm, rigid and crisp if they are to hold their shape while being covered with a desiccant. One of the main reasons for loss of form in preserved flowers is the attempt to preserve those which are showing signs of wilting. Discard any flowers marred by insect holes; distorted petals; unsightly marks or bruises (often a result of wind or rain damage); loss of colour or scorching caused by sun bleaching. If for some reason you cannot preserve flowers as soon as they are picked, re-cut the stems, to ensure intake of water, and immediately stand them in water. Keep them in the water until you can preserve them, but remember that flowers left in water for any length of time will continue to open.

A word of warning—do not expect to be able to store flowers in a freezer until you have time to preserve them—you may have heard or read of freeze-drying, but that is something completely different; it is a specialized process requiring elaborate equipment not generally available to the amateur. You know how dahlias in the garden look after the first hard autumn frost; well, this is exactly what your flowers will be like when you remove them from the freezer. You may argue, as many a telephone caller has with me, that you have put them in the freezer, and they look fine. Yes, I agree, they will look perfect while they are still frozen, but when you remove them and allow them to thaw out you can expect to encounter a soggy mass.

Transporting flowers

Although ideally flowers should be taken directly from the garden to the preserving tin, naturally this is not always possible, particularly for those without gardens, who have to rely on visits to friends' gardens, or florists. Flowers can usually be kept fresh and firm enough to withstand a journey if they are either stood in a container of water or water-retaining flower foam, or carefully placed in a refrigerator bag or box, provided that they are adequately protected from the moisture of the ice pack. Although flowers must be kept fresh they must also be kept dry, so it is unwise to pack them in a polythene bag—the moisture that forms on the inside of the bag will condense on the flowers.

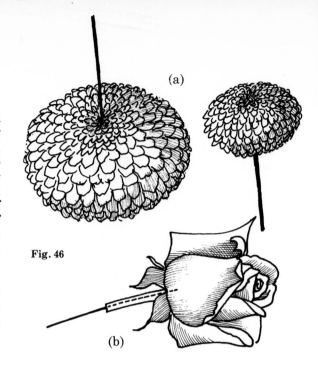

(a)

Fig. 46

(b)

Reviving wilted flowers

Should it be necessary to preserve flowers that have already wilted, they can often be revived by conditioning (a firming process). Fill a container with very warm to hot (but not boiling) water. Re-cut the flower stems as shown in fig. 45, then immediately plunge the ends into water. Let the flowers stand for several hours in a cool place. If for some reason you have had to pick flowers that ideally need to open a little more, they can be treated in the same way, but watch them carefully—do not leave them overnight, they may open too much while you sleep.

Wiring flowers

Some flowers, such as delphiniums, have stems which will remain firm and rigid after preservation. It would be ideal if all flowers were like this, but many, dahlias and water lilies, for example, have very succulent stems which will collapse when the moisture is drawn out, and so they need to have their stems replaced by florists' wires (fig. 46a). Other flowers, such as roses, which appear to have stiff stems, tend to develop a weakness just under the flower head which causes the head to flop

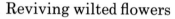

Fig. 45

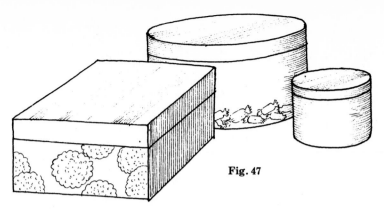

Fig. 47

over after preserving. This problem can be overcome by cutting the flower with about 40 mm ($1\frac{1}{2}$ in) of stem and pushing a wire up into the stem to reinforce it (fig. 46b). The best wires to use are 20-gauge, but if these are difficult to obtain, wires of a similar thickness will do. It is important to wire flowers before preserving. During the preserving process the sap in the flower will cause a corrosion of the wire, and this together with the slight shrinkage of the flower will ensure that when the flower is preserved the wire will remain firm and secure. At this stage it is only necessary to have a short length of wire—50 mm (2 in) or so. It is easier to fit flowers with short wires into preserving tins, and they are also easier to handle during the preserving process and easier to store. When you are ready to arrange the flowers the wire can be lengthened as shown in fig. 2, page 23.

Containers

For flower preservation with silica gel or preserving crystals gather together a selection of airtight tins in different shapes and sizes (fig. 47). It is often possible to buy large empty biscuit or sweet tins at confectioners' or big stores for a nominal sum—

especially at Christmas time. Small tins, particularly round ground coffee tins, are useful for preserving individual blooms. For borax preserving, you will need open cardboard boxes, so collect empty boxes, such as shoe boxes and chocolate and writing paper boxes.

It is very important that the correct type of container is used. To prepare your container, spoon desiccant into the bottom of the tin or box to form a layer approximately 12 mm ($\frac{1}{2}$ in) deep (fig. 48).

Positioning flowers

I recommend that the beginner should only attempt to preserve one layer of flowers in each tin, to avoid the risk of damaging the flowers. It is also advisable for the beginner to restrict each batch to one type of flower, to make it easier to calculate preserving times.

Fig. 48

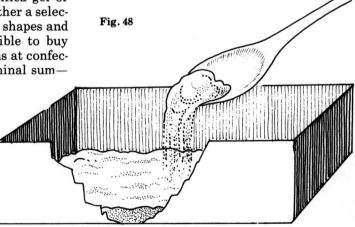

Fig. 49 (a)

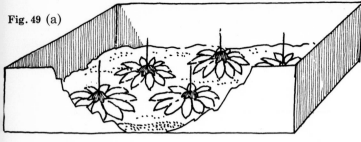

A face-down position (fig. 49a) is generally best for simple flowers with flat faces, such as daisies, which are the ideal type of flower for the beginner's first experiments. Clusters and sprays of florets should also be positioned in this way.

A face-up position (fig. 49b) is the most successful position for rounded double flowers and is particularly suitable for roses. It is also an alternative method for flat-faced flowers which are only partially open.

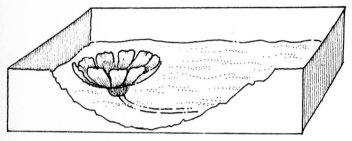

Flowers which are trumpet- or bell-shaped (individual hollyhock flowers, for example) should be positioned on their sides (fig. 49c).

Flower spikes, such as those of the delphinium, with florets encircling the entire stem, need a little extra protection if the florets are not to be crushed. An effective method is to bend two strips of thin cardboard tent-fashion, cut notches in them and place them in the bottom of the tin. The flower spikes can then be laid across the cardboard tent shapes, with their stems held in the notches (fig. 49d).

(b)

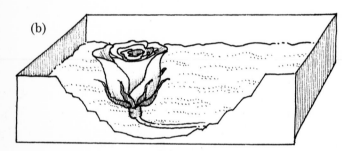

Covering the flowers

Preserving crystals and silica gel

(c)

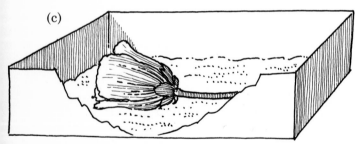

Using a large spoon, sprinkle preserving crystals slowly and carefully round each flower. Never sprinkle crystals on top of a flower, as the instant weight would destroy the flower's natural form. As you continue sprinkling, the crystals will cover the flowers (fig. 50a). Do not try to poke or force crystals in between the petals, this is not necessary and would cause damage and distortion. Exceptions to this rule are trumpet- or bell-shaped flowers, which should have their centres filled with crystals before crystals are sprinkled round them.

(d)

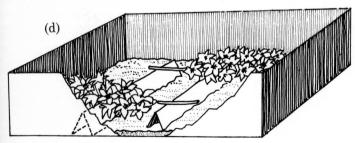

When flowers are completely covered, with a layer of crystals about 12 mm ($\frac{1}{2}$ in) deep on top, replace the lid of the tin (fig. 50b). If the lid is not completely airtight, seal it with sticky tape.

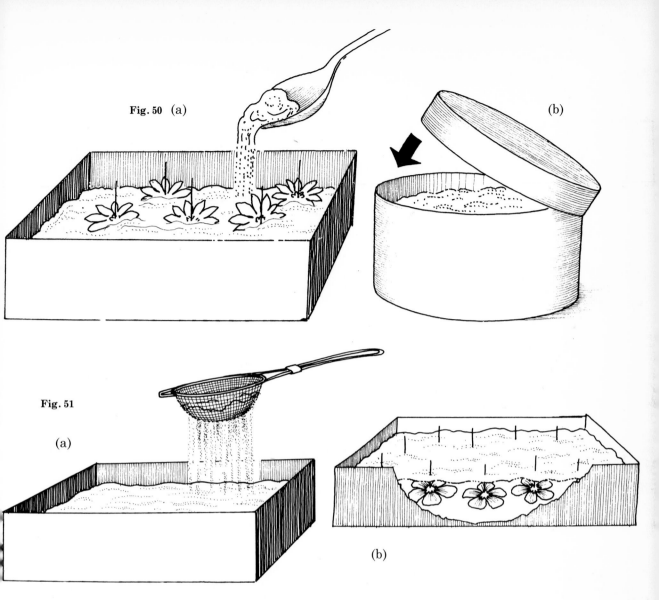

Fig. 50 (a)

(b)

Fig. 51

(a)

(b)

Borax

It is a good idea to sift borax over the flowers through a sieve, to disperse any remaining lumps in the powder (fig. 51a). You can sift the borax on top of the flowers—unlike crystals, borax will not crush them. If you prefer to spoon on the borax in the same way as preserving crystals, sieve it immediately before use. Again, the flowers should be covered with a 12 mm ($\frac{1}{2}$ in) layer (fig. 51b).

When the plant materials are completely covered, place the box, without a lid, where a constant temperature of 24°C (75°F) can be maintained—a heated airing cupboard is ideal.

Marking

It is essential that each tin or box should be clearly marked with its contents and the date. Failure to do this invariably causes chaos, especially if several batches are being preserved at different times. The length of time the flowers take to preserve will depend on the size, density and thickness of their petals. Many tiny flowers used in miniature arrangements only take two or three days, but larger flowers such as roses and dahlias take a week to ten days. Most will be preserved within two weeks, although very fleshy flowers, such as orchids, will take longer.

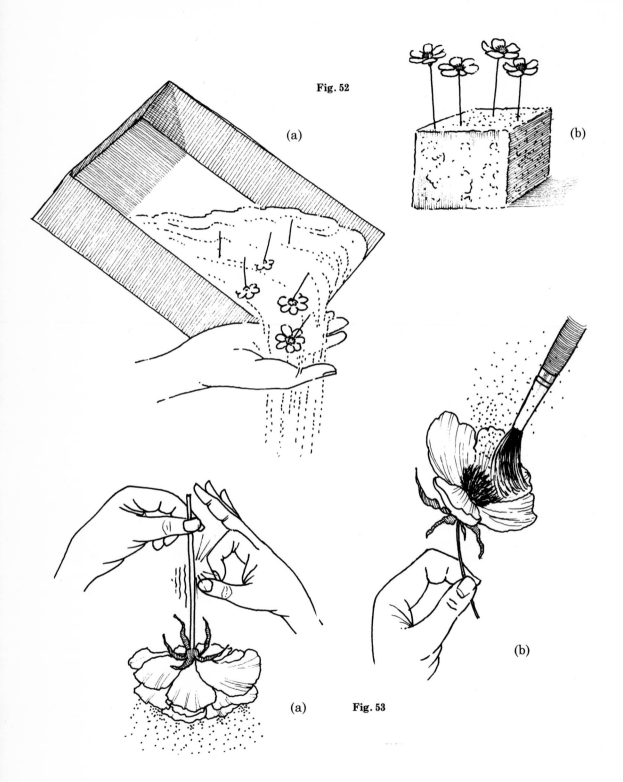

Fig. 52

(a)

(b)

(a)   **Fig. 53**

(b)

Removing flowers

Before attempting to uncover the complete batch, it is advisable to scrape back the desiccant gently and remove one flower. Hold the flower to your ear and give it a gentle flick; if it is ready, it will sound crisp and papery. The remaining flowers can then be removed by carefully pouring off the desiccant, letting it fall slowly through your fingers; this will enable you to catch each flower in turn and carefully remove it by its stem (fig. 52a). Stand the preserved flowers in a container or block of flower foam (fig. 52b), *never* pile them in a heap on the table.

Grooming

If specially prepared and selected crystals are used, these should fall away from most flowers as each one is removed from the tin, leaving the surface of the petals completely clean. A quick flick on the stem is all that is necessary to remove any residue (fig. 53a). Flowers with tiny hairs or rough surfaces in their centres may retain some particles, but these can easily be brushed away with a soft paintbrush (fig. 53b). A brush will also remove any clinging particles of borax.

Dealing with problems

When flowers, particularly of single-flowered varieties, are removed from the desiccant, the occasional petal will break off at the joint. If a dab of quick-drying contact adhesive is applied to the base of the petal it can be fixed securely back in place with little effort. Petals with very pointed bases can be attached more firmly if the bases are trimmed as shown in fig. 54 before they are glued back.

When moisture is removed from a flower there is always a slight shrinkage, which is usually most noticeable in single flowers and flowers with large petals. This means that petals which do not overlap become slightly spaced. It is advisable to give the petals a little artificial support by glueing the petals one to another, as shown in fig. 55.

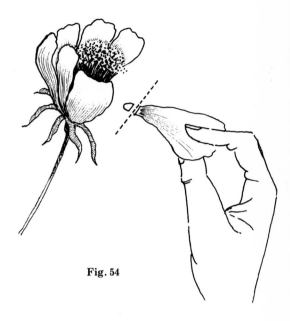

Fig. 54

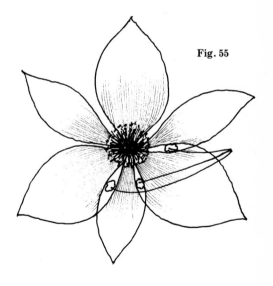

Fig. 55

149

Protection from damp

Flowers differ so much in structure and texture that it is really only when the arranger has preserved and handled many different types of flowers that a knowledge is acquired of how different flowers withstand damp weather conditions. Flowers suitable for preserving by the air method (see page 157) are usually unaffected, and so too are many desiccant-preserved flowers, particularly those with especially tough-textured petals or those, such as Pompon and decorative type dahlias, with small, closely packed, overlapping petals. Flowers with large petals are generally inclined to flop, although, again, much depends on the texture of the petals. In general, it is essential that desiccant-preserved flowers should be kept as dry as possible. Damp is a hazard I all too often have to contend with when transporting flower arrangements betwen my home and flower arrangement societies on a wet day. The encounters with the elements necessary to pack and unpack the car can spell disaster to the most carefully preserved flowers. Within the home, conditions are not so extreme, but we must avoid placing flowers in a room which is known to be damp. Even in centrally heated rooms, flowers susceptible to reabsorption of air moisture can be vulnerable during damp weather conditions in summer, when the heating is turned off. A coating of a specially prepared spray (fig. 56) can be very helpful for problem flowers, but it must only be applied to flowers when they are completely dry, that is, either as soon as the flowers are removed from the desiccant or taken from the storage tin (see page 160 for details of a suitable spray). It is important that the directions on such products should be carefully observed, as too heavy an application of spray can have a more disastrous effect than the damp weather conditions. When correctly applied the spray can also improve the flower visually, giving the petals a natural-looking sheen without making them too shiny. Varnish can also be used to give protection from damp. It is a matter of choice, but I feel varnish gives the flowers a very artificial look.

Never attempt to mix desiccant-preserved flowers with fresh foliage. This would mean that the flowers had to stand in water or water-retaining material, which would be disastrous to them.

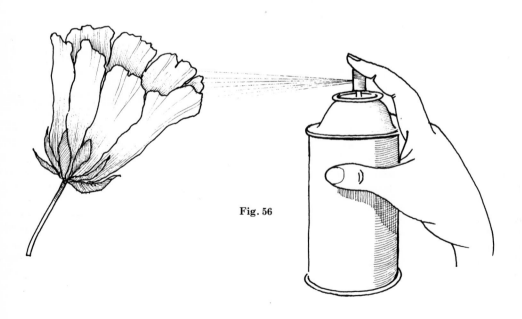

Fig. 56

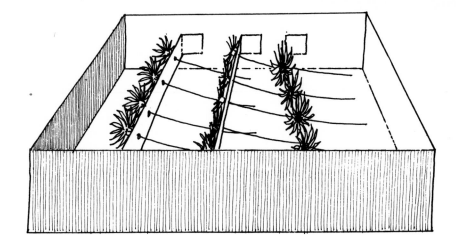

Fig. 57

Storage

Once flowers have been preserved they can be kept in absolutely perfect condition for many months if they are properly stored. Desiccant-preserved flowers should be stored either in flower foam in containers on the top shelf of a heated airing cupboard, or, alternatively, in sealed airtight tins. As a safety measure, before placing flowers in a tin, sprinkle a layer of dry desiccant in the bottom to absorb any air moisture in the tin, and also any moisture that may still remain deep down in the centres of the flowers. Cut strips of cardboard and pierce them with holes large enough to hold the flower stems. Glue the strips across the tin, as shown in fig. 57, and slip the flower stems through the holes. Replace the airtight lid—if you are in any doubt about whether the lid is completely airtight, it is advisable to seal it with sticky tape. Remember to mark the outside to indicate its contents. Store the tin in any convenient place where there is no danger of its being knocked over.

How long will desiccant-preserved flowers keep?

At demonstrations, exhibitions and in fact anywhere the subject of preserving is discussed, I am continually being asked how long preserved flowers will keep. Alas, it is a question to which there is no straightforward, simple answer. So many factors must be taken into consideration: room temperature, lighting, extent of handling, but mainly which flowers you have chosen to preserve. All flowers preserved with silica or borax must be treated with care; pretend each one is a delicate piece of porcelain. Only an arrangement covered by a glass dome or protected by the glass of a picture frame will retain its original degree of perfection for an indefinite period. But many preserved flowers in unprotected arrangements will keep their colour for years; I have flowers that are at least ten years old and still full of colour. And flowers whose colourings have become somewhat faded over the years can still be extremely useful when you want to create special colour effects, as several of my arrangements illustrate.

151

Preserving leaves with desiccants

The method for preserving leaves with desiccants is basically the same as for preserving flowers. There are just one or two points to note.

Round or oval-shaped leaves which have a naturally flattish habit of growth can be coaxed into more interesting forms by temporary wiring. Mould the leaf into the form you want and bind it with florists' fine silver binding wire, as shown in fig. 58. This can only be attempted before the leaves are preserved, while they are supple and can be manipulated easily without damage. After preserving the wire can be carefully removed and the leaves will retain their new shape. If necessary the leaves can also be wired in the same way as shown on page 18.

Because leaves are less intricate in their formation than flowers, it is easy to preserve several layers in a single tin; however, each layer of leaves must be covered with about 12 mm ($\frac{1}{2}$ in) of desiccant before the next layer is positioned (fig. 59).

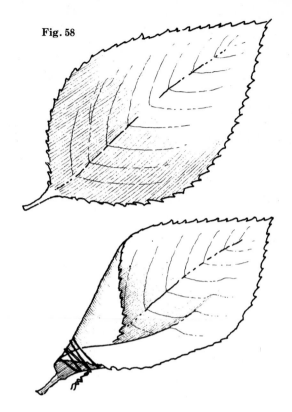

Fig. 58

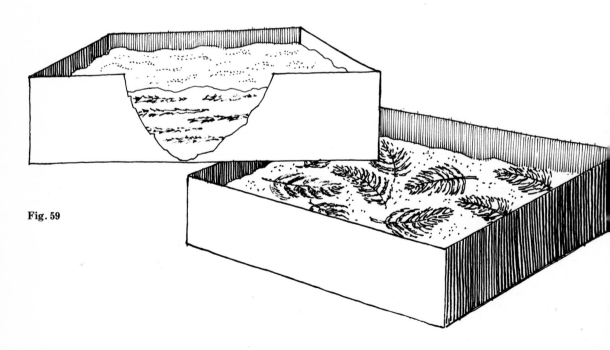

Fig. 59

152

Preserving with glycerine

Glycerine is a colourless and odourless syrupy liquid which when diluted with water becomes clear and is readily absorbed by plant material. It can be purchased from chemists' shops and drug stores. The glycerine method is most successfully used to preserve foliage. Leaves remain beautifully supple, but there will be a noticeable colour change. Plates 3 and 4 show examples of foliage which has been preserved by the glycerine method. They illustrate the range of colourings that can be obtained from leaves which when fresh are basically green.

Selecting and preparing foliage

The glycerine method is suitable for both evergreen and deciduous foliage, but it is important only to use it for fully mature foliage, as immature foliage will not preserve successfully. Most deciduous foliage reaches maturity by the end of June. It is equally important to gather deciduous foliage before the leaves develop their autumn tints, at which stage they will not be able to absorb the mixture. Both the immature deciduous leaves of spring and the beautiful shades of autumn leaves can be preserved by the desiccant method (see page 152).

When you gather branches of foliage for preserving, do not just cut them at random: look at each branch carefully and select only those of a suitable shape for the type of arrangement you are intending to create. Make sure the leaves are in good condition—not diseased or full of insect holes.

Check cut foliage and trim away any damaged leaves and any unwanted cross twigs. Thin out areas where the leaves are overcrowded.

Preparing a glycerine mixture

Add one part of glycerine to two parts of hot water (fig. 60) and mix them well together until the mixture looks clear. Gly-cerine is heavier than water, and unless you mix thoroughly the glycerine will remain at the bottom and only the water will be taken up by the foliage.

Pour the mixture to a depth of about 75 mm (3 in) into a container which is just large enough to take the foliage. For support, stand this container inside a larger container, such as a bucket, which is heavy enough to prevent the foliage toppling it over (fig. 61a). Woody-stemmed foliage should be split (fig. 61b) and put into the

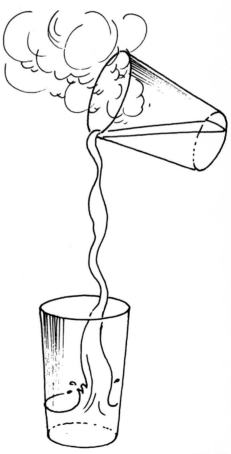

Fig. 60

hot mixture immediately after cutting. During a delay of even five minutes the base of the stem will seal over and will need to be re-cut to ensure an effective intake of the mixture. I feel sure that delay between cutting and putting the foliage into the mixture is often the cause of failure when preserving by this method. I find that another common mistake is to stand foliage in plain water for a period of time, allowing it to become so charged with water that the rapid intake of glycerine mixture necessary to ensure successful preserving will not be possible. This is a natural mistake for flower arrangers to make, as if foliage is to last well when it is used fresh in an arrangement it must of course be conditioned with water.

During the preserving process large individual leaves, such as fatsia leaves, have a tendency to flop at the point where the leaf joins the stem and this restricts absorption of the glycerine mixture. With leaves like this it is a good idea to support the joint with a stick secured to the centre of the leaf and stalk with pieces of adhesive tape (fig. 61c). Alternatively, you can use the tape to form a collar round the cupped leaf (fig. 61d). The leaf can then be placed lower down in the container so that the rim of the container supports it.

(a)

Fig. 61

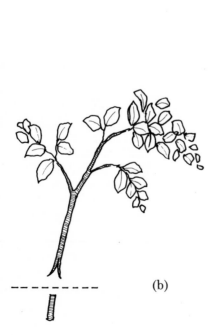

(b)

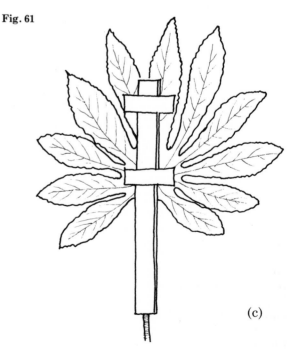

(c)

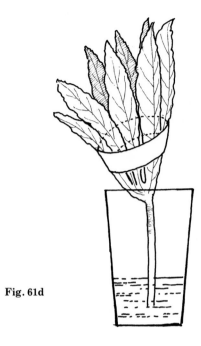

Fig. 61d

stage of preserving to complete the process with maybe a little left over, but the beginner should check the level of the mixture daily and top up with more mixture if necessary.

It is interesting to watch the glycerine mixture travelling through the leaves and observe the gradual change of colour. As an experiment, try removing some evergreen foliage when the mixture has been only partially taken through the leaves.

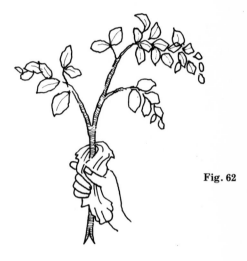

Fig. 62

Leave your container of foliage to stand in a warm, dry place, away from direct light. In recent years I have discovered that foliage will take up the glycerine mixture more successfully in a warm atmosphere than under cool conditions.

The time taken to preserve leaves varies according to several important factors. First, the texture and thickness of the leaves; naturally, thin-textured leaves require less time to preserve than thicker ones. Secondly, the temperature of the surrounding environment; the mixture is taken up more quickly in a warm room than a cool one. Thirdly, the time of year and even the time of day that the foliage is gathered often seems to make a difference to how quickly or slowly it takes up the mixture. Thin-textured leaves such as cotoneaster and escallonia will usually be ready in about four days, while tough, leathery leaves such as eleagnus or laurel may take three to four weeks.

Experience will enable the reader to give the foliage enough mixture in the initial

They may not remain quite so supple, but you will experience some interesting variations of leaf shadings.

Be sure to wipe the stems dry as soon as the plant materials are removed from the glycerine mixture (fig. 62). A common fault in the unsuccessful use of the glycerine method is to over-glycerine. Foliage requires the intake of only sufficient mixture to retain its supple texture and prevent the leaves from becoming shrivelled. Too much glycerine will result in the leaves feeling oily, often with tiny droplets of mixture visible on the surface of each leaf which can also encourage mildew to form. Leaves that are saturated with glycerine are also inclined to become floppy at the joint where the leaf stalk joins the stem.

Grooming

I think that probably the leaves of evergreen shrubs and trees are the most useful for preserving by the glycerine method, but evergreen leaves, particularly those, such as mahonia and eleagnus, which have large, flat surfaces, can present a problem. Because of the long growing period of these leaves, the accumulation of dust and grime on the surface of mature leaves can be quite considerable; and this is even more noticeable after preserving, giving the leaves a dull, lifeless appearance. However, after cleaning with a spot of oil they immediately become bright and gleaming and fresh-looking. The difference in appearance could be likened to the difference between a polished and an unpolished piece of furniture.

I find that practically any clear liquid oil is suitable for this purpose. For most people the obvious and most accessible oil will be the cooking oil from the kitchen. Apply just a spot of oil to a clean, soft cloth, and wipe over the entire surface of each leaf (fig. 63). Now wipe over the surface of each leaf again, using a clean, dry part of the cloth; if necessary repeat this process, until all the oily residue is removed and the leaves feel quite dry. Wiping with oil is also an ideal way of reviving preserved leaves that have been in store for a long time.

Preserving calyces and seedheads with glycerine

I often preserve calyces by a variant of the glycerine method. It is not suitable for calyces which consist of brightly coloured sepals—hydrangeas, for example. These should be preserved by the water method described on page 159. But generally it seems to give more lasting and therefore more successful results than the usual air method. It would also be a useful method to adopt for any seedheads that tend to become brittle when preserved by the air method. The mixture and the plant materials are prepared in exactly the same way as for preserving leaves, but the materials are only given a twenty-four to forty-eight hour drink of the mixture, just enough to secure the calyces, seeds or seedcases firmly on the stem, and to render them more supple and therefore easier to handle.

It is of the utmost importance that calyces should be mature before they are treated by either this method or the air method. A common fault is to try to preserve immature calyces, particularly of Bells of Ireland, which will not retain their shape successfully. If a calyx is mature, it will be firm to the touch. It may, however, be necessary even so to cut out the immature tip of each spike after preserving, as in cooler climates the spike rarely matures to the very tip.

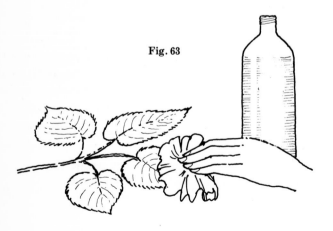

Fig. 63

A note on economy

Many people are tempted to throw away left-over glycerine mixture; this is very wasteful. It may have become discoloured, but I find that this does not affect its preserving qualities. Strain it through a fine sieve to remove any debris or even lumps of mould. (Mould will occasionally develop on the surface if the mixture has been allowed to stand for some time after use.) Reheat the mixture when it is needed and use it as before.

Preserving with anti-freeze

I am often asked about the use of anti-freeze for preserving. Personally I prefer to use glycerine; however, yes, anti-freeze is suitable for preserving, but only if the anti-freeze is glycerine-based. Follow the method for glycerine preserving, but do not dilute the anti-freeze. The colours of foliage preserved in anti-freeze can be expected to differ from those of glycerine-preserved foliage, but, after all, it is fun to experiment.

Storage

Although glycerine-preserved plant materials must be kept dry during storage, it is not advisable to enclose them completely. With a quantity of glycerine-preserved materials a certain amount of moisture is present, particularly if the intake of glycerine has been excessive. For this reason, plastic or polythene bags and boxes should not be used. If the place in which the plant materials are stored is subject to marked temperature changes condensation may develop on the inside of the plastic, as a result of which mildew will quickly form. Such conditions are often experienced in attics, which for many people is the obvious if not the only storage space.

Ideal containers for glycerined foliage are the cardboard boxes in which florists receive their fresh flower orders; these usually have holes in the sides which will allow air to circulate freely. As these boxes are usually discarded, florists are often more than willing to give them away. Alternatively, any strong cardboard box in which holes can be cut is quite suitable. Glycerined seedheads and calyces, particularly Bells of Ireland, will become squashed if they are kept in boxes and should either be hung up or stood in jam jars.

Most glycerine-preserved foliage will last, in fact evergreen leaves, which have a firmer texture than deciduous ones, will keep for many years. However, if storage conditions are particularly hot and dry the glycerine present in some thin-textured deciduous foliage, such as beech leaves, may dry out, causing the leaves to shrivel.

Air or natural preserving

Air or natural preserving is the easiest and simplest of all the methods of preserving. No special equipment or preservatives are required, just a basic understanding of what will successfully preserve by this method, when to gather it and where to preserve it.

What to preserve

Most of the colour in preserved plant material is provided by flowers and foliage which need to be preserved by either desiccants or glycerine. But everlasting flowers, which provide strong clear colours, and also a group of plants with small florets (see page 20) can be successfully preserved by the air method. Many flowers have interesting and decorative calyces which can also be preserved by this method. However, they will require careful handling, as when dry the calyces have a tendency to break away from the stem. Personally, I prefer to preserve them by the glycerine treatment described on page 156; there is then a more lasting bond between calyx and stem. Seedheads form by far the largest group of plant materials for which the air method is suitable.

As neither complicated nor time-consuming methods are required for air preserving, there is a great temptation to gather large quantities of one type of plant material, for instance seedheads, all small and round. This is fine if they are needed, but arrangers who are preserving for their own pleasure are usually well advised to be selective and gather smaller quantities of a wider variety of plant materials, concentrating all the time on contrasting shapes, forms and textures.

When to gather

Of the everlasting flowers it is important to note that statice should be fully open before gathering, while helichrysums should be gathered just as they begin to open. If they

157

are left until they are fully open they look unattractive and will most probably explode to release their seeds. Helichrysums also need to be wired as soon as they are gathered (see page 144). Helichrysums gathered after maturity can be retrieved and used to make fun flowers (see page 103).

Decorative calyces should be fully mature, so that they feel firm to the touch, before they are gathered.

See page 24 for the stages at which seedheads can be gathered. Particular attention should be paid to seedheads with seeds directly attached to the stem rather than being contained in a case or pod. Wild dock is a typical example of such a seedhead. It is essential that these are gathered when they are fully formed but before they reach maturity, by which stage they will have lost their colouring and will rapidly shed their seeds.

Sort through the plant materials and discard any that are damaged or malformed. Any leaves which are attached to the stems will need to be removed, as even if they are still fresh and green they will become too shrivelled and brittle to be of any use. I suggest that large leaves that come away easily should be removed at this stage, but smaller leaves will break away much more easily after they have dried, in fact really tiny ones will just rub off.

Gather plant materials into small bunches and secure them with plastic-covered wires (fig. 64). As the stems dry and shrink these can be tightened much more easily than string. I have discovered that the plastic-covered wires sold as garden ties are the perfect length for this purpose; alternatively, freezer bag ties can be used.

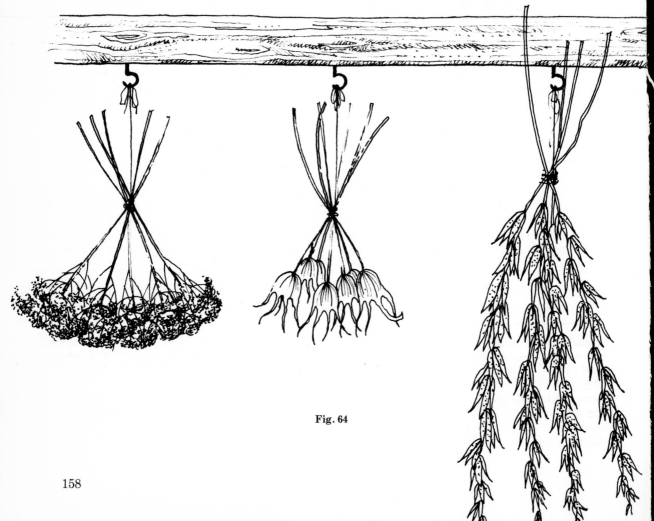

Fig. 64

Where to preserve

Hang plant materials heads down in a dry, airy and dark place. Most plant materials to be preserved by this method will do best in cool conditions, but the preserved colourings of some flowers may be richer if the flowers are hung in a warm place, for example, an airing cupboard. If hanging facilities with these conditions are difficult to find, many of the suggested plant materials can be stood in weighted jam jars (fig. 65). Plant materials which do not have rigid stems can be encouraged to develop graceful curves if they are allowed to stand rather than hang.

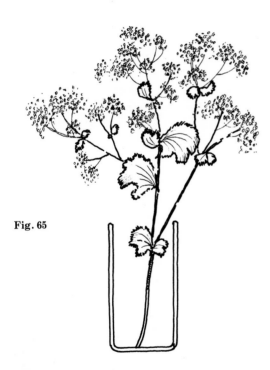

Fig. 65

Arrange and preserve

Mature hydrangeas can be preserved very easily and successfully by the following method. Pick only those which already feel dry and slightly papery to the touch. Re-cut and slit the stems, then immediately stand or arrange them in about 25 mm (1 in) of water (fig. 66). Allow them to take up this water, then dry out. No further water should be added. I must emphasize that hydrangeas have to be fully mature to preserve successfully by this method. Hydrangeas gathered during the summer can only be preserved by the desiccant method. But the arranger in a hurry might like to experiment with this method for other flowers and calyces.

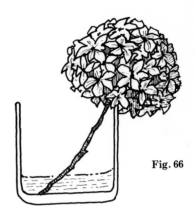

Fig. 66

Nature's gleanings

In our efforts to collect and preserve interesting plant materials we should not overlook those which the elements have already preserved for us. There are occasions when these gleanings can be as useful to the flower arranger as instant convenience foods are to the busy cook. Gathered in late autumn or early winter, the skeleton structure of seedheads can be the inspiration for an arrangement, or, maybe, a fun flower.

Natural preserving can certainly not be recommended as a successful way of preserving most foliage—the majority of leaves, certainly of the deciduous varieties of trees and shrubs, lose their shape and just shrivel. However, the texture and structure of the leaves of many evergreen trees and shrubs enable old leaves to retain their shape and develop quite pleasant muted shades of brown as they fall and continue their process of dying under the tree.

Acknowledgements

There are always many people who contribute to the publication of a book and I would like to express my thanks to all concerned. However, I would like to say a special 'thank you' to the following people:

Russell Bennet, Editor of *Flora* Magazine for his kind permission to include plates 14, 25, 26, 28, 81, 82, 83.

Pemberton Somerville Ltd, Interior Decorators, 16 West Street, Wilton, Salisbury, for the loan of fabrics used in plates 7, 27, 28, 31.

Miss Mary Pritty for typing my manuscript. Collins Publishers who have given me this opportunity to share with my readers my love and enthusiasm of the natural beauty and colour that preserved plant materials can bring to all of us in our homes.

Suppliers

Flora Products, Stanley Gibbons Ltd, Drury House, Russell Street, London WC2B 5HD
Send a stamped addressed envelope for containers, floral art scissors and other accessories for flower arrangers.

M. F. Crystals, 77 Bulbridge Road, Wilton, Salisbury, Wiltshire SP2 0LE
Send a stamped addressed envelope for details of specially prepared flower preserving crystals and Flora-Seal (a special spray to seal and protect flowers).